TEXAS

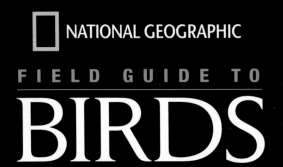

NATIONAL GEOGRAPHIC

FIELD GUIDE TO

BIRDS

TEXAS

NATIONAL GEOGRAPHIC

FIELD GUIDE TO

BIRDS

Edited by JONATHAN ALDERFER

National Geographic
Washington, D.C.

Introduction

Texas is one of the places that birders dream of visiting. Ecologically diverse with deserts in the west and pine forests in the east, it is a crossroads of the bird world. There have been a staggering 629 species documented for the state, about 450 of which can be found every year. Of course, it would take a lot of traveling to see them all in a single year.

The ecological diversity of Texas can be seen by heading eastward along Interstate Highway 10 from El Paso to Orange. El Paso is in the Chihuahuan Desert, with only eight inches of precipitation annually, where birds such as Crissal Thrashers and Black-throated Sparrows can be found. Far West Texas is dominated by desert habitats, but there are also larger mountain ranges that provide islands of woodland habitat. Each range is unique with varied and interesting bird life. The Colima Warbler is found in the United States only in the pine and oak woodlands of the Chisos Mountains in Big Bend National Park. East of this region is the Texas hill country. The oak and juniper woodlands of this region are home to the Golden-cheeked Warbler, which nests nowhere else in the world. Further eastward are the Blackland Prairie and oak savannahs of east-central Texas, then the coastal prairies. The Texas coast is well known as a place for migrant birds to rest and feed on their way northward. Next are the great pine forests of the Southeast where specialty species such as the Red-cockaded Woodpecker reside. Other regions of the state include the High Plains where Lesser Prairie-Chickens still strut and the lower Rio Grande Valley, which is home to many tropical species such as the Green Jay and Altamira Oriole.

Texas is a fascinating place which has much to offer anyone interested in studying birds, and the best part is that all areas of the state have something to offer.

MARK LOCKWOOD
Co-Author, *Handbook of Texas Birds*

FRONTISPIECE: LITTLE BLUE HERON WADING
PHOTO BY BATES LITTLEHALES

CONTENTS

KIOWA AND
RITA BLANCA
NATIONAL
GRASSLAND

HIGH

BLACK
KETTLE
N.G.

PLAINS

Canadian

LAKE MEREDITH
N.R.A.

McCLELLAN
CREEK N.G.

R
O
C
K
Y

Amarillo

BUFFALO LAKE N.W.R.

PALO DURO
CANYON
S.P.

NEW
MEXICO

M
O
U
N
T
A
I
N
S

MULESHOE
N.W.R.

Lubbock

L L A N O

E S T A C A D O

Abilene

U.S.
MEXICO

El Paso

T   E

GUADALUPE MTS.
NATIONAL
PARK

Pecos

Rio Grande

BALMORHEA
S.P.

E D W A R D S

P L A T E A U

DAVIS
MOUNTAINS
S.P.

CHIHUAHUA

AMISTAD
N.R.A.

BIG BEND
NATIONAL
PARK

Amistad
Reservoir

KICKAPOO
CAVERN
S.P.

Rio Grande

COAHUILA

M E X I C O

NUEVO
LEÓN

MAP KEY

National Park
National Monument, NAT. MON.
National Preserve, NAT. PRES.
National Recreation Area, N.R.A.
National Seashore

National Forest, N.F.

National Grassland, N.G.

National Wildlife Refuge, N.W.R.

State Park, S.P.
State Natural Area, S.N.A.

State boundary

Dam

State capital

Point of interest

SELECTED BIRDING SITES
OF
TEXAS

OKLAHOMA

ARKANSAS

Red
Lake Texoma
Red

Wichita Falls

HAGERMAN N.W.R.

CADDO NATIONAL GRASSLAND

LYNDON B. JOHNSON N.G.

Fort Worth
Dallas

Brazos

Trinity

Toledo Bend Reservoir

X   A   S

Leon

MERIDIAN S.P.

Waco

DAVY CROCKETT N.F.

SABINE N.F.

LOUISIANA

Colorado

Llano

BALCONES CANYONLANDS N.W.R.

SAM HOUSTON N.F.

ANGELINA N.F.

PEDERNALES FALLS S.P.

Austin

BIG THICKET NAT. PRES.

Sabine

ATTWATER PRAIRIE CHICKEN N.W.R.

Beaumont
Houston

McFADDIN N.W.R.

LOST MAPLES S.N.A.

San Antonio

Guadalupe

BRAZOS BEND S.P.

TEXAS POINT N.W.R.
ANAHUAC N.W.R.
GALVESTON ISLAND S.P.
BRAZORIA N.W.R.
SAN BERNARD N.W.R.
BIG BOGGY N.W.R.

Frio

ARANSAS N.W.R.

Matagorda Bay

GOOSE ISLAND S.P.

Nueces

King Ranch

Corpus Christi

Gulf of Mexico

Laredo

PADRE ISLAND NATIONAL SEASHORE

Falcon Reservoir

miles
0   100   200

BENTSEN-RIO GRANDE VALLEY S.P.

McAllen

LAGUNA ATASCOSA N.W.R.

0   100   200
kilometers

SANTA ANA N.W.R.

Brownsville

TAMAULIPAS

LOOKING AT BIRDS

What do the artist and the nature lover share? A passion for being attuned to the world and all of its complexity, via the senses. Every time you go out into the natural world, or even view it through a window, you have another opportunity to see what is there. And the more you know what you are looking at, the more you see.

Even if you are not yet a committed birder, it makes sense to take a field guide with you when you go out for a walk or a hike. Looking for and identifying birds will sharpen and heighten your perceptions, and intensify your experience. And you'll find that you notice everything else more acutely—the terrain, the season, the weather, the plant life, other animal life.

Birds are beautiful, complex animals that live everywhere around us in our towns and cities, and in distant places we dream of visiting. Here in North America more than 900 species have been recorded—from abundant commoners to the rare and exotic. A comprehensive field reference like the *National Geographic Field Guide to the Birds of North America* is essential for understanding that big picture. If you are taking a spring walk in the Texas countryside, however, you may want something simpler: a guide to the birds you are most likely to see, which slips easily into a pocket.

This photographic guide is designed to provide an introduction to the common birds—and a few rare birds—you might encounter in Texas: how to identify them, how they behave, and where to find them, with specific locations.

Discovery, observation, and identification of birds can be exciting, whether you are a novice or expert. As an artist and birder for most of my life, I know that every time I go out to look at birds, I see more clearly and have a greater appreciation for the natural world around me and my own place in it.

JONATHAN ALDERFER
Editor

National Geographic Field Guide to Birds: Texas is designed to help beginning and practiced birders alike quickly identify birds in the field. The book is organized by bird families, following the order in the *Check-list to the Birds of North America*, by the American Ornithologists' Union. Families share structural characteristics, and by learning these shared characteristics early, birders can establish a basis for a lifetime of identifying birds and related family members with great accuracy—sometimes merely at a glance. (For quick reference in the field, use the color and alphabetical indexes at the back of this book.)

A family may have one member or dozens of members, or species. In this book each family is identified by its common name in English along the right-hand border of each spread. Each species is also identified in English, with its Latin genus and species—its scientific name—found directly underneath. One species is featured in each entry.

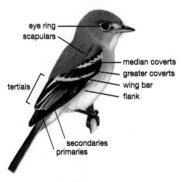

eye ring
scapulars
median coverts
greater coverts
wing bar
flank
tertials
secondaries
primaries

Least Flycatcher

supercilium
postocular stripe
ear patch (auricular)
moustachial stripe
submoustachial stripe

median crown stripe
lateral crown stripe
supraloral area
lores
malar stripe

Lark Sparrow

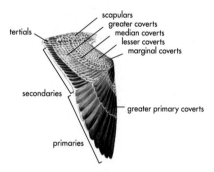

tertials

scapulars
greater coverts
median coverts
lesser coverts
marginal coverts

secondaries

greater primary coverts

primaries

Great Black-backed Gull, upper wing

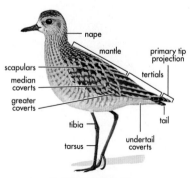

nape
mantle

primary tip projection

scapulars
median coverts
greater coverts

tertials

tibia
tarsus

tail

undertail coverts

Pacific Golden-Plover

An entry begins with **Field Marks**, the physical clues used to quickly identify a bird, such as body shape and size, bill length, and plumage color or pattern. A bird's body parts yield vital clues to identification, so a birder needs to become familiar with them early on. After the first glance at body type, take note of the head shape and markings, such as stripes, eye rings, and crown markings. Bill shape and color are important as well. Note body and wing details: wing bars, color of primary flight feathers, wing color at rest, and shape and markings when extended in flight. Tail shape, length, color, and banding may play a big part, too. At left are diagrams detailing the various parts of a bird— its topography—labeled with the term likely to be found in the text of this book.

The main body of each entry is divided into three categories: Behavior, Habitat, and Local Sites. The **Behavior** section details certain characteristics to look or listen for in the field. Often a bird's behavioral characteristics are very closely related to its body type and field marks, such as in the case of woodpeckers, whose chisel-shaped bills, stiff tails, strong legs, and sharp claws enable them to spend most of their lives in an upright position, braced against a tree trunk. The **Habitat** section describes areas that are most likely to support the featured species. Preferred nesting locations of breeding birds are also included in many cases. The **Local Sites** section recommends specific refuges or parks where the featured bird is likely to be found. A section called **Field Notes** finishes each entry, and includes information such as plumage variations within a species; or it may introduce another species with which the featured bird is frequently confused. In either case, an additional drawing may be included to aid in identification.

Finally, a caption underneath each of the photographs gives the season of the plumage pictured, as well as the age and gender of the bird above, if differentiable. A key to using this informative guide and its range maps follows on the next two pages.

READING THE SPREAD

1 Photograph: Shows bird in habitat. May be female or male, adult or juvenile. Plumage may be breeding, molting, nonbreeding, or year-round.

2 Caption: Defines the featured bird's plumage, age, and sometimes gender, as seen in the picture.

3 Heading: Beneath the common name find the Latin, or scientific, name. Beside it is the bird's length, and frequently its wingspan. Wingspan is given with birds often seen in flight. Female measurements are given if disparate from male.

4 Field Marks: Gives basic facts for field identification: markings, head and bill shape, and body size.

5 Band: Gives the common name of the bird's family.

6 Range Map: Shows year-round range in purple, breeding range in red, winter range in blue. Areas through which species are likely to migrate are shown in green.

7 Behavior: A step beyond **Field Marks**, gives clues to identifying a bird by its habits, such as feeding, flight pattern, courtship, nest-building, or songs and calls.

8 Habitat: Reveals the area a species is most likely to inhabit, such as forests, marshes, grasslands, or urban areas. May include preferred nesting sites.

9 Local Sites: Details local spots to look for the given species.

10 Field Note: A special entry that may give a unique point of identification, compare two species of the same family, compare two species from different families that are easily confused, or focus on a historic or conservation fact.

On each map of Texas, range boundaries are drawn where the species ceases to be regularly seen. Nearly every species will be rare at the edges of its range. The sample map shown below explains the colors and symbols used on each map. Ranges continually expand and contract, so the map is a tool, not a rule. Range information is based on actual sightings and therefore depends upon the number of knowledgeable and active birders in each area.

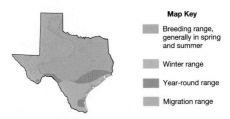

Map Key

Breeding range, generally in spring and summer

Winter range

Year-round range

Migration range

Sample Map: Blue-Gray Gnatcatcher

READING THE INDEXES

There are two indexes at the back of this book. The first is a **Color Index** (p. 262), created for birders to make quick IDs in the field. In this index, male birds are labeled by their predominant color: Mostly White, Mostly Black, etc. Note that a bird may have a head of a different color than its label states. That's because its body—the part most noticeable in the field—is the color labeled.

The **Alphabetical Index** (p. 266) is organized by the bird's common name. Next to each entry is a check-off box. Most birders make lists of the birds they see. Some keep several lists, perhaps one of birds in a certain area and another of all the birds they've ever seen—a life list. Such lists enable birders to look back and remember their first sighting of an Indigo Bunting or an American Kestrel.

Year-round | Adult

FULVOUS WHISTLING-DUCK

Dendrocygna bicolor L 20" (51 cm)

FIELD MARKS
Rich tawny head and underparts; white rump; black tail

Black back feathers edged in tawny buff; dark blue bill

Dark line down hindneck, continuous in female, broken in male

Behavior
More active at dusk and night than during the day, often traveling in small, noisy flocks from daytime roosts to feeding areas. Feeds both by dabbling and by diving for aquatic plants and seeds. In flight, extends neck and feet past body, more like a swan or goose than a duck. Call is a squealing, whistled *pe-chee*, usually heard in flight.

Habitat
Forages in shallow, marshy fields especially those associated with agricultural operations. Also found in open country and coastal plains. Roosts during the day in thick vegetation. Also nests on the ground in thick vegetation of marshes.

Local Sites
The Fulvous Whistling-Duck nests locally along the entire Gulf Coast. A good place to look in summer is Anahuac National Wildlife Refuge.

FIELD NOTES The Black-bellied Whistling- Duck, *Dendrocygna autumnalis* (inset), a close relative of the Fulvous, is distinguished by its gray face, black belly, red bill, and white wing patch. Its call, a high, whistled *pe-che-che-nee,* is longer than that of the Fulvous. It can be found year-round at Santa Ana National Wildlife Refuge.

Year-round | Adult white morph

SNOW GOOSE

Chen caerulescens L 35" (89 cm) W 45" (114 cm)

FIELD MARKS
White overall or, less commonly,
dark gray-brown; black primaries
show in flight

Heavy pinkish bill with black
"grinning patch"

Juvenile is dingy gray-brown on
head, neck, and upperparts

Behavior
Travels in huge flocks, especially during fall migration.
Loud, vocal birds, sounding like baying hounds, flocks
fly in loose V-formation and long lines, sometimes
more than 1,500 miles nonstop, reaching speeds up to
40 mph. Primarily vegetarian, forages on agricultural
grains and plants and on all parts of aquatic vegetation.
An agile swimmer, commonly rests on water during
migration and at wintering grounds. Listen for its
harsh, descending *wouk,* heard continuously in flight.

Habitat
Most often seen on grasslands, grainfields, and coastal
wetlands, favoring standing shallow freshwater marshes
and flooded fields. Breeds in the Arctic.

Local Sites
Snow Geese winter in huge flocks the length of the Gulf
Coast and in large portions of the Panhandle. Flocks of
up to 100,000 birds can be found foraging through the
rice fields around Attwater Prairie Chicken National
Wildlife Refuge.

FIELD NOTES Amid a flock of Snow Geese, look as
well for the smaller, less common Ross's
Goose, *Chen rossii* (inset). It is set apart by a
stubby, triangular bill and a shorter neck.

Year-round | Adult

CANADA GOOSE

Branta canadensis L 30-43" (75-108 cm) W 59-73" (148-183 cm)

FIELD MARKS
Black head and neck marked with
distinctive white chin strap

In flight, shows large, dark wings,
white undertail coverts, and a
long protruding neck

Variable gray-brown breast color

Behavior
A common, familiar goose in winter; best known for
migrating in large V-formation. Its distinctive musical
call of *honk-a-lonk* makes it easy to identify, even without seeing it. It also makes a murmuring sound when
feeding, and a hissing sound when protecting young.
Like some other members of its family, the Canada
Goose finds a mate and remains monogamous for life.
Family groups tend to stay together through the winter.

Habitat
Prefers wetlands, grasslands, and cultivated fields
within commuting distance of water. It has adapted
successfully to man-made habitats such as golf courses
and farms, to the extent that it sometimes chases off
other nesting waterbirds.

Local Sites
The Canada Goose can be found throughout Texas in
winter from Aransas National Wildlife
Refuge on the coast to Buffalo
Lake in the Panhandle.

FIELD NOTES Ongoing research
into the mitochondrial DNA of the Canada
Goose has found that the smaller subspecies, such as *hutchinsii*
(inset, left) and *minima* (inset, right), actually belong to their own
species, the newly named Cackling Goose, *Branta hutchinsii*.

Breeding | Adult male

WOOD DUCK

Aix sponsa L 18½" (47 cm)

FIELD MARKS
Male has glossy iridescent head
and crest, lined in white; red,
white, black, and yellow bill; bur-
gundy breast with white spotting

Female duller overall with large
white teardrop-shaped eye patch

Squared-off tail shows in flight

Behavior
Most commonly feeds by picking insects from the
water's surface or by tipping into shallows to pluck
invertebrates from the bottom, but may also be seen
foraging on land. The omnivorous Wood Duck's diet
changes throughout the year depending upon available
foods and its need for particular proteins or minerals
during migration, breeding, and molting. Male Wood
Ducks give a soft, upslurred whistle when swimming.
Female Wood Ducks have a distinctive rising, squealing
flight call of *oo-eek*.

Habitat
Prefers woodlands and forested swamps. Nests in tree
cavities or man-made nest boxes. Will sometimes nest
some distance from water if cavities are scarce.

Local Sites
A fairly common species year-round on lakes through-
out the pine woods of eastern Texas. Look for the
Wood Duck in Brazos Bend State Park near Houston.

FIELD NOTES The Wood Duck hen hatches up to 15 eggs in
a single clutch in cavities high up in trees or nest boxes. Once
hatched, the young must make a long jump to the water, sometimes 30 feet below. Protected by their downy newborn
plumage, they generally splash down safely.

Breeding | Adult male

MALLARD

Anas platyrhynchos L 23" (58 cm)

FIELD MARKS
Male has metallic green head and
neck, white collar, chestnut breast

Female mottled brown overall;
orange bill marked with black

Both sexes have bright blue
speculum bordered in white; white
tail and underwings

Behavior
A dabbler, the Mallard feeds by tipping into shallows
and plucking seeds, grasses, or invertebrates from the
bottom. Also picks insects from the water's surface. The
courtship ritual of the Mallard consists of the male
pumping his head, dipping his bill, and rearing up in
the water to exaggerate his size. A female signals
consent by duplicating the male's head-pumping.
Listen for the female Mallard's loud, rasping quack.

Habitat
This widespread species occurs wherever shallow fresh
water is to be found, from coastal lagoons to urban
ponds. May be found in winter in some salt marshes
and bays. Nests on the ground in concealing vegetation.

Local Sites
Mallards winter across much of Texas, becoming more
common farther north. Breeding pairs can be found at
Buffalo Lake and Muleshoe National Wildlife Refuges.

FIELD NOTES At first glance, the
green head of the male Northern
Shoveler, *Anas clypeata* (inset,
right), can be mistaken for the Mallard's.
Look for the Shoveler's large, dark, spatulate bill—a telltale
mark on both the drake and hen (inset, left). The Northern
Shoveler winters throughout Texas.

Year-round | Adult male, left; adult female, right

MOTTLED DUCK

Anas fulvigula L 22" (56 cm)

FIELD MARKS
Mottled brown body; paler head
with unstreaked throat and face

Faint streaking on back of head
and neck; greenish blue speculum

Male's bill a bright yellow;
female's a duller orange

Behavior
Pairs or small family groups forage mainly for insects,
crustaceans, small fish, and mullosks, but also tip over
in shallows for aquatic plants. Family groups remain
together except during postbreeding dispersal. Courtship begins early in winter while Mallards are still
present, and hybridization is increasing where ranges
overlap. Female's quack is similar to female Mallard's;
male emits raspy *kreeeb kreeeb kreeeb.*

Habitat
This nonmigratory bird prefers coastal salt marshes
and ponds in coastal prairies. Nests in dense marsh
grasses, always relatively near a body of water.

Local Sites
Found year-round along the Gulf Coast, any of the
coastal refuges are likely to house a pair, from Laguna
Atascosa to Anahuac National Wildlife Refuge.

FIELD NOTES The female Mallard (inset) is
easily confused with the Mottled
Duck in winter when both can be
found along the coast. The Mallard
hen is a lighter brown, with a more heav-
ily streaked face, a white tail, and a considerable amount
of black on her bill.

Breeding | Adult male

BLUE-WINGED TEAL

Anas discors L 15½" (39 cm)

FIELD MARKS

Male has violet-gray head with white crescents on sides, spotted brown body, and white flank patch

Female has mottled brown body with paler head

Both genders have light blue forewing patches visible in flight

Behavior

Flies rapidly in tight, twisting flocks. A dabbling duck, it feeds on surface insects or tips into water to eat aquatic plants, seeds, and small crustaceans. Like other dabblers, also called "puddle ducks," does not require a running start to take off, but can spring directly into flight. Female gives a hoarse quack; male makes a high, sibilant note in flight.

Habitat

Prefers freshwater marshes, ponds, and lakes in open country. Nests on the ground, often in a prairie.

Local Sites

A common and widespread spring and fall migrant throughout Texas, the Blue-winged Teal can be found breeding in the Panhandle at sites like Muleshoe National Wildlife Refuge, or wintering along the southern coastal plain at sites like Aransas National Wildlife Refuge.

FIELD NOTES Though one of the smaller ducks in North America, some Blue-winged Teals are known to travel up to 7,000 miles during migration between subarctic breeding grounds and tropical wintering grounds.

Breeding | Adult male

REDHEAD

Aythya americana L 19" (48 cm)

FIELD MARKS
Male has light back and sides, black breast and tail, rufous head

Female is brown overall with a patch of white below the bill

Bill is blue-gray with white ring and black tip

Behavior
Large flocks congregate into "floating rafts" in winter, feeding mostly at dawn and dusk by diving for aquatic vegetation. Flies with strong wing beats in a V-formation. On more northerly breeding grounds, hens deposit their eggs in the nests of other waterfowl species, sometimes even in bittern nests. Female's call is a rough, grating *squak*.

Habitat
Winters on large lakes, bays, estuaries, and coastal lagoons, often mixed with other species.

Local Sites
Found in winter on large bodies of water throughout Texas. Huge numbers can be found at Laguna Atascosa National Wildlife Refuge, widely considered one of the Redhead's most important wintering locales.

FIELD NOTES The closely related Canvasback, *Aythya valisineria* (inset: male, left; female, right), is often a victim of the Redhead's brood parasitism on their shared breeding grounds from the northern Great Plains to Alaska. The Canvasback drake's head is a deeper maroon and his back and sides are white; the hen has a dusky brownish gray body. Both have solid black bills.

Breeding | Adult male

LESSER SCAUP

Aythya affinis L 16½" (42 cm)

FIELD MARKS
Black head has a slightly peaked
crown, sometimes purplish gloss

Black neck and breast, black tail;
black-and-white barred back;
white sides

Female has brown head, neck,
upperparts; white at base of bill

Behavior
One of North America's most abundant diving ducks,
due perhaps to its varied diet, the Lesser Scaup forages
on aquatic insects, mollusks, and crustaceans. Will dive
to bottom to sift through the mud while swimming.
Also consumes snails, leeches, and small fish, and will
forage for seeds and vegetation. Listen for the female's
unusual rattled purr.

Habitat
Large flocks can be found wintering in sheltered bays,
inlets, lakes, and rivers. Also wanders inland to
agricultural fields and marshes.

Local Sites
A winter resident of the entire length of Texas. Both
Lesser and Greater Scaup can be found by November at
Hagerman National Wildlife Refuge on the Red River.

FIELD NOTES The Greater Scaup, *Aythya
marila* (inset: male, left; female,
right), very closely resembles
the Lesser in both sexes.
The Greater's more
rounded head is its most distinguishable field mark. Look as well
for its larger bill with a broader black tip. The larger amount of
white on the Greater Scaup's wings is another helpful field mark.
The Greater Scaup is more common in the eastern half of Texas.

Breeding | Adult male

BUFFLEHEAD

Bucephala albeola L 13½" (34 cm)

FIELD MARKS
Small duck with large puffy head, steep forehead, and short bill

Male has large white head patch and a glossy black back

Female is gray-brown overall with small, elongated white patches on either side of her head

Behavior
Often seen in small flocks, some birds keeping a lookout on the water's surface while others dive for aquatic insects, snails, and small fish. Like all divers, the Bufflehead's feet are set well back on its body to swiftly propel it through the water. Able to take off directly out of water, unlike many other diving ducks. Truly monogamous, Buffleheads are believed to stay with the same mate for years and to faithfully return to the same nesting site each season. Male's call is a squeaky whistle, female emits a harsh quack.

Habitat
Found on sheltered bays, rivers, and lakes in winter. Breeds for the most part in Canada.

Local Sites
The Bufflehead commonly winters on bodies of water throughout the state, arriving in late October and departing by early May, though some coastal birds begin migration in early April.

FIELD NOTES In its boreal forest breeding grounds in Canada, this smallest of North American diving ducks nests almost exclusively in cavities created by the Northern Flicker; a nesting site so tiny that it is speculated to have influenced the Bufflehead's own small size.

Year-round | Adult male

RUDDY DUCK

Oxyura jamaicensis L 15" (38 cm)

FIELD MARKS
Brown-gray upperparts, pale
underparts with brown barring

Male has bright white cheeks;
female's cheeks crossed by single
dark line

Juvenile resembles female
through its first winter

Behavior
Referred to as a "stiff-tail" from its habit of cocking its
tail upright, this small, chunky diver has a grebe-like
ability to sink beneath the surface of water and disappear from view, its stiff tail feathers serving as a rudder
as it forages. Adapted for diving, its feet are the largest
relative to body size of all ducks. With legs positioned
far back on its body, it can barely walk upright. Feeds
primarily on aquatic insects and crustaceans; eats little
vegetable matter. The Ruddy generally remains silent.

Habitat
Found in tightly clustered flocks on lakes, bays, and salt
marshes during migration and winter.

Local Sites
Common in the winter throughout Texas, look for
Ruddy Ducks on the ponds and sheltered bays of
Anahuac National Wildlife Refuge.

FIELD NOTES The shy and elusive Masked Duck, *Nomonyx
dominicus* (inset: female, left; male,
right), the only other North American stiff-
tailed duck, is a rare and irregular visitor to
Texas' Gulf Coast and lower Rio Grande Valley. Look for the
breeding male's black face and blue bill hidden in dense aquatic
cover of Anahuac or Santa Ana National Wildlife Refuges.

Nonbreeding | Adult

PLAIN CHACHALACA

Ortalis vetula L 22" (56 cm)

FIELD MARKS
Olive-brown above, grayer on
head and neck; dusky buff below

Dark greenish tail feathers are
broadly tipped with white

Patch of red skin on throat of
displaying male

Behavior
The only chachalaca that occurs in North America,
nests, roosts, and forages in trees, descending to the
ground for dust baths. Eats fruits, berries, green leaves,
tree buds, seeds, and occasionally insects. Small groups
of four to twenty birds can be seen half-hopping, half-
gliding from branch to branch. Eponymous call, *cha-
cha-lac*, is heard year-round, but especially while
breeding and especially at dusk and dawn.

Habitat
Inhabits tall chaparral thickets and wooded riparian
areas in its limited range. Nests in the fork of a tree or
in a dense bush.

Local Sites
Found in thickets along the lower Rio Grande River.
Santa Ana National Wildlife Refuge and Bentsen-Rio
Grande Valley State Park are good places to search for
this species any time of the year.

FIELD NOTES The loud, raucous call of the Plain Chachalaca is
unmistakable in early dawn when the vocalization of one will
elicit a response in another nearby and so on until the whole area
resounds with the cacophony.

Year-round | Adult

SCALED QUAIL

Callipepla squamata L 10" (25 cm)

FIELD MARKS
Grayish overall with dark edges of neck, breast, and belly feathers giving a scaled appearance

Crest tipped in white on male; shorter and buffier on female

Juvenile more rufous above, not as conspicuously scaled-looking

Behavior
Prefers to walk or run on the ground, rather than fly. Seen in pairs during breeding season, in large coveys at other times of year. Feeds on insects, seeds, flower blossoms, and fresh shoots. Generally spends day in the cool shade of a low shrub. Low, nasal *chip-churr* call, accented on the second syllable, is employed by pairs and coveys to keep together while foraging.

Habitat
Found in arid, semidesert scrublands, and grasslands mixed with scrub. Female builds nest on ground, sheltered by grasses or shrubs.

Local Sites
A year-round resident in arid regions of the Panhandle and West Texas, the Scaled Quail is likely to be found in the brushy scrub of Big Bend National Park.

FIELD NOTES The largest member of the closely related pheasant family, the Wild Turkey, *Meleagris gallopavo* (inset), is unmistakable with its dark, iridescent body, red wattle, and featherless head. Look for it foraging on the ground for seeds, nuts, and acorns in open areas of Buffalo Lake National Wildlife Refuge.

Breeding | Adult

LEAST GREBE

Tachybaptus dominicus L 9¾" (25 cm)

FIELD MARKS

Blackish overall; darkest on crown

Bright yellow eyes

Short, dark, thin bill; short neck

Throat is white, bill paler, head browner on nonbreeding birds

Behavior

The smallest grebe of North America. Hides in vegetation, foraging mainly for aquatic insects. Almost always seen in a pair, and will nest at any season on almost any quiet, inland piece of water. Adapts readily to newly formed bodies of water. Aggressively defends territory against other pairs of grebes with its loud, resonating, high-pitched cries.

Habitat

Stays near the weedy or marshy shores of ponds, sloughs, and ditches. Builds nest on still water, either floating or anchored by aquatic plants.

Local Sites

With a limited range that only enters the United States through Texas, the Least Grebe can be found on the lower coastal prairies and in the lower Rio Grande Valley at sites like Santa Ana and Laguna Atascosa National Wildlife Refuges.

FIELD NOTES The location of the Least Grebe's nest at the edge of a marshy pond or sometimes even in open water allows easy access for the birds, but protects the eggs and young from land-based predators. At least partially floating, the nest is also protected from small fluctuations in the water level.

Breeding | Adult

PIED-BILLED GREBE

Podilymbus podiceps L 13½" (34 cm)

FIELD MARKS
Small and short-necked

Breeding adult brownish gray
overall; black ring around stout,
whitish bill; black chin and throat

Winter birds lose bill ring; chin
becomes white; plumage is
browner overall

Behavior
The most widespread of North American grebes, the
Pied-billed remains for the most part on water, seldom
on land or in flight. When alarmed, it slowly sinks,
holding only its head above the water's surface. Its bill
allows it to feed on hard-shelled crustaceans, breaking
apart the shells with ease. Pursues fish underwater and,
once prey is grasped in its bill, will eat it whole while
still submerged. Lobed toes make grebes strong
swimmers. Call is a loud *cuk-cuk-cuk* or *cow-cow-cow*.

Habitat
Prefers nesting around freshwater marshes and ponds.
Also found in more open waters of large bays and
rivers, where it dives to feed on aquatic insects, small
fish, frogs, and vegetable matter. Winters on both fresh
and salt water.

Local Sites
A widespread species, the Pied-billed may be found in
winter on almost any body of water in Texas.

FIELD NOTES Like most grebes, including the Least, the Pied-
billed eats its own feathers and feeds them to its young, perhaps
to protect their stomach linings from fish bones or animal shells.

Breeding | Adult

BROWN PELICAN

Pelecanus occidentalis L 48" (122 cm) W 84" (213 cm)

FIELD MARKS
Exceptionally long bill with dark gray throat pouch

Silvery gray above; blackish brown below; white crown; pale yellow forehead

Breeding adult's hindneck is chestnut; winter adult's is white

Behavior
Dives from the air into water to capture prey. On impact, its throat pouch balloons open, scooping up small fish. Tilts its bill downward to drain water, tosses its head back to swallow. Sometimes gather in large groups over transitory schools of fish, attracting other seabirds to the feeding frenzy. Flocks travel in long, staggered lines, alternately flapping and gliding in unison. For years endangered, this species is currently making a significant recovery following a severe decline in its population due to pesticide poisoning.

Habitat
Largely coastal, the Brown Pelican makes its home along the shore in sheltered bays and near beaches. Breeds on islands in large stick nests.

Local Sites
These once endangered birds are now common at coastal sites such as Galveston Island and Goose Island State Parks.

FIELD NOTES The American White Pelican, *Pelecanus erythrorhynchos* (inset), shares the exceptionally long bill of the Brown Pelican, but is largely white with black flight feathers. It winters across Texas' coastal prairies and breeds on islands near Aransas National Wildlife Refuge.

Breeding | Adult

NEOTROPIC CORMORANT

Phalacrocorax brasilianus L 26" (66 cm) W 40" (102 cm)

FIELD MARKS
Black overall; bill hooked at tip

Dull yellow throat patch is
bordered in white

Long, black tail

Breeding adult acquires short,
white plumes on sides of neck

Behavior
Often seen perched on fence posts, trees, jetties, or
wires, sometimes with wings spread to dry in the sun.
With emerald eyes adapted to underwater vision, hunts
fish by diving from the surface. Also feeds on crustaceans and amphibians. Forms groups, beating water
with their wings in order to flush prey. Grunts and
croaks given mainly at nesting site.

Habitat
Found on lakes, rivers, and sheltered bays, in fresh,
brackish, or salt water. Nests on the ground on islands
or low in trees and shrubs over water.

Local Sites
Coastal sites like Galveston Island State Park and Aransas
National Wildlife Refuge are usually reliable for finding
Neotropic Cormorants, especially in sum-
mer before many move farther south.

FIELD NOTES Large flocks of Double-crested
Cormorants, *Phalacrocorax auritus* (inset), arrive
in winter onto the Neotropic's turf, displacing the
latter to areas farther south. The Double-crested
is larger, has a broader bill, a proportionately
shorter tail, and lacks a white border around its
throat patch. It is also much more widespread inland.

Breeding | Adult female

ANHINGA

Anhinga anhinga L 35" (89 cm) W 45" (114 cm)

FIELD MARKS
Black overall; long, black tail

Silvery white spots and streaks
on wings and upper back

Females have buffy neck
and breast

Long, sharply pointed bill

Behavior
Can control its buoyancy and often swims with its body
submerged and only its head above water. Hunts while
swimming underwater, spearing fish with long, sharp
bill, then tossing it into air to catch and swallow. Often
seen perched on branches or stumps near water, wings
outspread to dry in the sun. Roosts in trees overlooking
water. Though generally silent, makes rapid clicking
sound when engaged in a dispute.

Habitat
Prefers freshwater ponds, lakes, swamps, and slow-
moving rivers bordered by cypress trees or mangroves;
generally not found on coasts. Builds nest low in trees
or shrubs, or uses one made by an egret or heron.

Local Sites
Sites slightly inland from the coast and encompassing
extensive marshland and swamps, like Brazos Bend
State Park or Santa Ana National Wildlife Refuge, are
ideal spots to find the Anhinga sunning itself.

FIELD NOTES The Anhinga flies with slow, regular wing beats and
often soars at great heights on rising thermal columns of air like
a raptor, sometimes in flocks of 20 or more birds. When soaring,
it holds its wings perpendicular to its body, forming a perfect
cross with its small head and long tail.

Breeding | Adult

GREAT BLUE HERON

Ardea herodias L 46" (117 cm) W 72" (183 cm)

FIELD MARKS
Gray-blue overall; white foreneck
with black streaks; yellowish bill

Black stripe extends above eye

Breeding adult has plumes on its
head, neck, and back

Juvenile has dark crown; no plumes

Behavior
Often seen standing or wading along calm shorelines
or rivers, foraging for food. It waits for prey to come
into its range, then spears it with a quick thrust of its
sharp bill. Flies with its head folded back onto its
shoulders in an S-curve, typical of other herons as well.
When threatened, draws its neck back with plumes
erect and points its bill at antagonist. Sometimes emits
an annoyed, deep, guttural squawk as it takes flight.

Habitat
May be seen hunting for aquatic creatures in marshes
and swamps, or for small mammals inland, in fields
and forest edges. Pairs build stick nests high in trees in
loose association with other Great Blue pairs.

Local Sites
Common and widespread, the Great Blue Heron is
found throughout Texas year-round, but especially on
the coastal prairies and along shorelines.

FIELD NOTES The almost exclusively
coastal Tricolored Heron, *Egretta tricolor*
(inset), is nearly half the size of the Great Blue,
and its white belly and foreneck contrast sharply with its dark
blue upperparts. The Tricolored is known to actively give chase
to fish, sometimes in water up to its belly.

Breeding | Adult

GREAT EGRET

Ardea alba L 39" (99 cm) W 51" (130 cm)

FIELD MARKS
Large white heron with heavy
yellow bill, black legs and feet

Breeding adult has long plumes
trailing from its back, extending
beyond the tail

Blue-green lores while breeding

Behavior
Stalks its prey slowly and methodically, foraging in
shallow water with sharply pointed bill to spear small
fish, aquatic insects, frogs, and crayfish. Also known to
hunt snakes, birds, and small mammals. Occasionally
forages in groups or steals food from smaller birds.
Listen for the Great Egret's guttural croaking or its
repeated *cuk-cuk.*

Habitat
Common to both fresh and saltwater wetlands. The
Great Egret makes its nest in trees or shrubs 10 to 40
feet above the ground. Colonies may have as many
as a hundred birds.

Local Sites
Found in largest numbers along the coast and adjoin-
ing prairies, look for huge flocks in late summer at sites
like Anahuac and Aransas National Wildlife Refuges.

FIELD NOTES Early in the breeding season, the Great Egret grows
long, ostentatious feathers called aigrettes from its scapulars. In
the late 1800s, aigrettes were so sought after by the millinery
industry that Great Egrets were hunted nearly to extinction. The
grassroots campaign to end the slaughter later developed into
the National Audubon Society. Today, loss of wetlands continues
to limit the population of Great Egrets and other herons.

Nonbreeding | Adult

SNOWY EGRET

Egretta thula L 24" (61 cm) W 41" (104 cm)

FIELD MARKS
White heron with slender black
bill and legs; yellow eyes, lores,
and feet

Breeding adult has upward-
curving plumes on head, neck,
and back; nonbreeding adult
lacks plumes

Behavior
An active feeder, the Snowy Egret may be seen running
in shallows, chasing after fish, insects, and crustaceans.
Also forages by stirring up bottom water with feet to
flush out prey. In breeding display, the Snowy Egret
raises its plumage, pumps its head up and down, and
flashes the skin at the base of its bill, which has turned
from yellow to vermilion. Also during breeding season,
the generally quiet bird will bray gutturally, pointing its
bill straight up.

Habitat
Prefers wetlands and sheltered bays along the coastline.
Nests several feet up in trees among mixed colonies
including heron, egret, and ibis species.

Local Sites
Numbers of the Snowy Egret, like the Great Egret, tend
to be highest in summer along the immediate coastline
at sites like Anahuac and Aransas National Wildlife
Refuges. It is also a common migrant across the state.

FIELD NOTES In flight, the Snowy Egret can be easily confused
with either the smaller Cattle Egret or the larger Great Egret.
Look for its long, thin, black bill and its slender, black legs with
yellow feet that extend well beyond its body. Its wing beats are
considerably more rapid than the Great Egret's.

Nonbreeding | Adult

LITTLE BLUE HERON

Egretta caerulea L 24" (61 cm) W 40" (102 cm)

FIELD MARKS
Slate blue; dull green legs and
feet; blue-gray bill and lores

Adult in high breeding plumage
has reddish purple head and
neck, black legs and feet

Immature bird white with black
wing tips, grayish bill and lores

Behavior
A slow and methodical feeder, hunts for fish and small crustaceans. Strictly carnivorous, it snags its prey with its sharply pointed bill. Like all herons, the Little Blue may be seen preening its contour and flight feathers with its pectinate, or comblike, middle toes. Breeding male sings a distinctive *ee-oo-ah-ee-ee.* Both male and female emit hoarse croaks and squawks.

Habitat
Prefers freshwater ponds, lakes, and marshes, and coastal saltwater wetlands. Both sexes build nest of sticks and twigs low to the ground in a tree or shrub.

Local Sites
The Little Blue Heron nests throughout much of East Texas, including the wetlands of Brazos Bend State Park and Sam Houston National Forest.

FIELD NOTES The Little Blue Heron inhabits many of the same wooded wetlands as the usually solitary Green Heron, *Butorides virescens* (inset). The Green Heron is characterized by a deep chestnut neck and blue-green cap, back, and wings. It is one of the few tool users in the bird world, luring minnows within its range using twigs, insects, or earthworms.

Breeding | Adult dark morphs

REDDISH EGRET

Egretta rufescens L 30" (76 cm) W 46" (117 cm)

FIELD MARKS
Dark morph is dark gray overall
with rusty head and breast

White morph is entirely white

Pink bill with black tip, shaggy
plumes on head and neck

Immature gray, cinnamon markings

Behavior
Hunts for small fish by casting a shadow with its spread
wings, called "canopy feeding," or by startling prey into
the open by stirring up mud in shallow water. Often
lurches about, spins, dashes after elusive fish, and stabs
the water repeatedly while seeking a meal. Nests and
roosts in mixed colonies. Though usually silent, will
emit low croaks and grunts at nesting site.

Habitat
The Reddish Egret inhabits shallow, open salt pans and
mangrove swamps, preferring coastlines and islands.
Nests on the ground on a platform of sticks.

Local Sites
Tends to stay along the Gulf, generally in greater
numbers on the southern half of Texas' coastline.
Regularly, though rarely, visitors also make rounds to a
number of inland reservoirs as far west as Balmorhea
State Park.

FIELD NOTES The white morph of the Reddish Egret resembles
other white egrets, but is smaller than the Great Egret and larger
than the Snowy. Like the dark morph, its bill is pink with a black
tip, and its legs and feet are dark blue. The dark morph pre-
dominates in Texas with the white morph accounting for only
a small percentage.

Breeding | Adult

CATTLE EGRET

Bubulcus ibis L 20" (51 cm) W 36" (91 cm)

FIELD MARKS
Small, stocky, white heron with rounded head

Breeding adult has red-orange bill and orange-buff plumes on crown, back, and foreneck

Nonbreeding adult has yellow bill, yellowish legs

Behavior
Often seen among livestock in fields, feeding on insects flushed out by tractors, farm machinery, or grazing cattle—hence the name. When seeking a mate, a male aggressively establishes a territory and is then approached by a group of females, who bite his neck and back while he attempts to repel them. After three or four days, the male allows a female to stay. Mutual backbiting, stretching by the female, and twig-shaking by the male all occur, precursors to nest-building. Though silent for the most part, the Cattle Egret may emit a two-tone *rick-rack* sound on nesting grounds.

Habitat
Widespread and common in summer in open fields, on farms, and along highway medians. Nests in trees or shrubs, grouped into mixed-species heronries.

Local Sites
Not as tied to aquatic habitats as most egrets, the Cattle can be found year-round along the coast and at more inland sites like Hagerman National Wildlife Refuge during breeding season.

FIELD NOTES This Old World species came to South America from Africa in the 1870s, spread to Florida in the 1950s, and reached Texas by November 1955. Recently its population has declined in many areas of the United States.

Breeding | Adult

BLACK-CROWNED NIGHT-HERON

Nycticorax nycticorax L 25" (64 cm) W 44" (112 cm)

FIELD MARKS
Black crown and back

Two to three white hindneck plumes, longest when breeding

White underparts and face; gray wings, tail, and sides of neck

Immature streaked brown

Behavior
Primarily a nocturnal feeder. Even when feeding during the day, remains in the shadows, almost motionless, waiting for prey to come within range. Forages for fish, frogs, rodents, reptiles, mollusks, eggs, and nestlings. Black-crowneds, consumers of fairly large prey, are susceptible to accumulating contaminants; their population status is an indicator of environmental quality. Call heard in flight is a gutteral *quok*.

Habitat
This heron has adapted to a wide range of habitats, including salt marshes, brackish and freshwater wetlands, and lakeshores that provide cover and forage. Nests in colonies high up in trees.

Local Sites
Locally common throughout much of Texas, the nightherons are most evident at dusk at sites on Texas' coastal plain.

FIELD NOTES The adult Yellow-crowned Night-Heron, *Nyctanassa violacea* (inset), is also a nocturnal feeder adorned with long, white neck plumes. A head patterned in black and white and a largely gray body distinguish the Yellow-crowned from its cousin.

Year-round | Adult

Eudocimus albus L 25" (64 cm) W 38" (97 cm)

FIELD MARKS
White plumage and red facial skin

Long, reddish, decurved bill with
black tip; reddish legs and feet

Black tips of primaries in flight

Immatures have mostly brown
heads, necks, and backs

Behavior
Feeds in small groups, wading through shallow water
or marshland, thrusting its bill into soil to probe for
prey. Also sieves water for food with its bill. During
courtship, a mating pair rub their heads together, offer
grass and sticks to each other, and engage in mutual
preening. Gathers in dense breeding colonies in trees or
shrubs during spring and summer. Listen for the male's
hunk-hunk-hunk-hunk call.

Habitat
Abundant in coastal salt marshes and swamps. Also
found in coastal lagoons and croplands. Builds nests in
trees or bushes, often on islands offering protection
against predation.

Local Sites
Numbers of White Ibis in Texas have risen significantly
in the past few decades. They are especially abundant in
summer along the upper Gulf Coast.

FIELD NOTES The White-faced Ibis,
Plegadis chihi (inset), the only
representative of its family regularly
found in western Texas, shares such structural
characteristics with the White Ibis as a very
long, decurved bill and a long neck held straight forward in flight.
It is a glossy chestnut overall with red lores outlined in white.

Year-round | Adult

ROSEATE SPOONBILL

Platalea ajaja L 32" (81 cm) W 50" (127 cm)

FIELD MARKS
Large wading bird with distinctive
long spatulate bill

Unfeathered greenish head

Pink body with scarlet fringing on
wings and rump, orange tail

Juveniles paler pink

Behavior
Often seen in a small group, swinging its head from
side to side, sweeping its long, flat, partially open bill
through shallow water. When its sensitive bill brushes
against small fish or invertebrates, it immediately snaps
shut. Courting pairs rub heads together, offer grass and
sticks to each other, and engage in mutual preening. If
disturbed, the spoonbill emits soft quacking noises as it
takes flight; may also be heard at breeding colonies.

Habitat
Prefers shallow salt- and freshwater marshes and
lagoons. Nests in colonies on close strings of islands,
usually with other species of herons and egrets.

Local Sites
The Roseate Spoonbill can be found along barrier
islands and at slightly inland bodies of water along the
entire Gulf Coast, generally in greater numbers in
summer toward the northern portions of the coastline.

FIELD NOTES The spoonbill population was nearly extinguished
in the United States in the latter half of the 19th century due
to plume hunters who would at times wipe out entire colonies.
Recolonization efforts have contributed to a significant recovery,
but factors such as pollution and mosquito-control pesticides
still threaten their preferred habitats.

Year-round | Adult

TURKEY VULTURE

Cathartes aura L 27" (67 cm) W 69" (175 cm)

FIELD MARKS

In flight, two-toned underwings contrast and long tail extends beyond feet

Brownish black feathers on body; silver-gray flight feathers

Unfeathered red head; ivory bill; pale legs

Behavior

An adept flier, the Turkey Vulture soars high above the ground in search of carrion and refuse. Rocks from side to side in flight, seldom flapping its wings, which are held upward in a shallow V, allowing it to gain lift from conditions that would deter many other raptors. Well developed sense of smell allows the Turkey Vulture to locate carrion concealed in forest settings. Feeds heavily when food is available but can go days without if necessary. Generally silent.

Habitat

Hunts in open country, woodlands, farms, even in urban dumps and landfills. Often seen over highways, searching for roadkill. Nests solitarily in abandoned buildings or hollow logs and trees.

Local Sites

Both vultures are abundant year-round across the eastern half of Texas.

FIELD NOTES The Black Vulture, *Coragyps atratus* (inset), is not as efficient at finding a meal, but just as aggressive. It will sometimes follow a Turkey Vulture to its find and claim it as its own. Unfeathered heads and hooked bills aid both species in consuming carrion.

Year-round | Adult

WHITE-TAILED KITE

Elanus leucurus L 16" (41 cm) W 42" (107 cm)

FIELD MARKS
Long, pointed wings with dark
"thumb" mark; long, mostly white
tail and white underparts

Black shoulder patches show as
black leading edges in flight

Juvenile head and underparts
lightly streaked rufous

Behavior
Hovers while hunting, with tail down and legs
dangling, hanging motionless in the wind like its
namesake: the kite. On sighting prey, swoops down to
clutch it in its strong talons. Feeds primarily on small
rodents, lizards, and insects. Mainly seen alone during
the day, but roosts communally by night. Can soar long
distances on few wing beats once it has caught a
thermal, a rising current of warm air. Call is a brief,
whistled *keep keep keep*, uttered mainly near the nest.

Habitat
Fairly common in ranchlands, prairies, and marshland,
where scattered brush provides perches. Both sexes
build nest of sticks and grasses in trees or yucca plants.

Local Sites
Most common along the lower Gulf Coast north to
about Corpus Christi, Laguna Atascosa National
Wildlife Refuge is a reliable spot year-round.

FIELD NOTES This rather small bird of prey can, from a distance,
be mistaken for a gull. In flight, look for its sharply pointed wings,
its dusky primaries, and its characteristic dark spot toward the
tip of its wing linings, commonly referred to as its "thumb" mark.
In addition, no gull can hover quite as gracefully and adeptly as
the White-tailed Kite.

Juvenile

COOPER'S HAWK

Accipiter cooperii L 14-20" (36-51 cm) W 29-37" (74-94 cm)

FIELD MARKS
Blue-gray upperparts; reddish
bars across breast, belly

Dark gray cap; bright red eyes

Long, rounded, barred tail with
white terminal band

Juvenile brown with yellow eyes

Behavior
Usually scans for prey from a perch, then attacks with
a sudden burst of speed. Flies fast and close to the
ground, using brush to conceal its rapid attack. The
Cooper's is the raptor most likely to snatch a chicken
from a farm. Also feeds on other birds, rabbits, rodents,
reptiles, and insects. Known to hold prey underwater to
drown it. Uses a *kek-kek-kek* call at nest site.

Habitat
Prefers broken, especially deciduous, woodlands and
streamside groves. Has also adapted to fragmented woodlands created by urban and suburban development.

Local Sites
An uncommon winter resident throughout the state.
Pedernales Falls State Park is a good place to spot the
Cooper's year-round.

FIELD NOTES Distinguishing a Cooper's from a Sharp-
shinned Hawk, *Accipiter striatus* (inset: juvenile,
left; adult, right), is one of birding's more difficult
identifications. Both species are largely brown
as juveniles; blue-gray above, barred rufous
below as adults. The Sharp-shinned is slightly
smaller, has a more squared-off tail, and its neck
does not extend as far in flight.

Year-round | Adult

WHITE-TAILED HAWK

Buteo albicaudatus L 23" (58 cm) W 50" (127 cm)

FIELD MARKS
Rusty shoulders contrast with
dark gray upperparts

White underparts and chin; short
white tail with single black band

At rest, long, broad wings extend
well beyond tail

Behavior
This Texas specialty spots prey from perch or in flight,
hunting primarily for rabbits, but also rodents, reptiles,
frogs, and large insects. Known to converge on grass
fires in order to feed on prey flushed by the flames. Will
occasionally eat carrion. Reuses and rebuilds same nest
site year after year. Though generally silent, alarm call
at nest is a high-pitched *ke-eh, ke-eh, ke-eh, ke-eh.*

Habitat
Inhabits open coastal grasslands and semiarid inland
brush country of southern Texas. Nests of sticks and
grasses found atop low trees or yucca plants.

Local Sites
This raptor's range only enters the United States in
southern coastal Texas, for the most part south of
Matagorda Bay at sites such as King Ranch or
Laguna Atascosa National Wildlife Refuge.

FIELD NOTES Another raptor of semiarid brushland in
southern Texas is the Harris's Hawk, *Parabuteo
unicinctus* (inset). Like the White-tailed Hawk, its
rusty chestnut shoulder patches contrast with
darker upperparts, but the Harris's dark brown
underparts and chestnut wing linings and leggings
sharply distinguish it. It also has a noticeably longer tail
with a broader black band than the White-tailed.

Year-round | Adult

RED-TAILED HAWK

Buteo jamaicensis L 22" (56 cm) W 50" (127 cm)

FIELD MARKS
Brown above; red tail on adults

Whitish belly with broad band of dark streaking

Dark bar on leading edge of underwing

Immature has brown, banded tail

Behavior
Watch the Red-tailed Hawk circling above, searching for rodents, sometimes kiting, or hanging motionless on the wind. Uses thermals to gain lift and limit its energy expenditure while soaring. Perches for long intervals on telephone poles and other man-made structures, often in urban areas. Listen for its distinctive call, a harsh, descending *keee-eeer*.

Habitat
Seen in more habitats than any other North American buteo, from woods to prairies to deserts. Common at habitat edges, where field meets forest or wetlands meet woodlands, favored for the variety of prey found there.

Local Sites
Common throughout the state. Scan the edges of open areas for a perched Red-tailed surveying its territory.

FIELD NOTES Five subspecies of Red-tailed Hawk regularly occur in Texas. The widespread *borealis* race, described above, is a year-round resident throughout East Texas. The western *calurus* race is washed with rufous below. The paler *fuertesi* race, sometimes lacking a breast band, can be found in most of South Texas. The even paler *krideri* race, always lacking a breast band, moves into Texas in winter. Finally, the blackish *harlani* race, a winterer in East Texas, has a dusky white tail with no red at all.

Year-round | Adult

CRESTED CARACARA

Caracara cheriway L 23" (58 cm) W 50" (127 cm)

FIELD MARKS
Blackish brown overall, with white throat and neck, barred breast

Red-orange to yellow facial skin

Shows whitish patches near the ends of long, rounded wings

Tail has black terminal band

Behavior
Also known as the "Mexican Eagle," soars on long, flat wings in flapping, raven-like flight. Forages on the ground in search of earthworms, insects, lizards, small mammals, and nestlings. Feeds on carrion, often in the company of vultures. Though usually silent, calls include a low rattle and a single *wuck* note. At nest, listen for a loud *wik-wik-wik-wik-kerr*, on the last note of which the bird will throw its head over its back.

Habitat
Inhabits prairies, ranchlands, and mesquite brushlands. Nests atop a low tree or a tall yucca plant.

Local Sites
Resides primarily in the lower Rio Grande and southerly coastal areas of Texas. Laguna Atascosa National Wildlife Refuge is a good spot to find a nesting pair, though they are to be found locally as far north as the Dallas area.

FIELD NOTES The Crested Caracara is the only North American member of the family *Falconidae* that builds a nest, often atop yucca plants that line the lower Rio Grande Valley. Both sexes help to build the bowl-shaped nest out of sticks, vines, and twigs, and both parents participate in the incubation and feeding of the young.

Year-round | Adult male

AMERICAN KESTREL

Falco sparverius L 10½" (27 cm) W 23" (58 cm)

FIELD MARKS
Russet back and tail; streaked
tawny to pale underparts

Two black stripes on white face

Male has blue-gray wing coverts

Female has russet wing coverts

Behavior
Feeds on insects, reptiles, mice and other small
mammals. Hovers over prey by coordinating its flight
speed with the wind speed, then plunges down for the
kill. Will also feed on small birds, especially in winter.
Regularly seen perched on fences and telephone lines,
bobbing its tail with frequency. Has clear, shrill call of
killy-killy-killy.

Habitat
North America's most widely distributed falcon, found
in open country and in cities, often mousing along
highway medians or sweeping down the shoreline.
Nests in tree holes or barns using little nesting material.

Local Sites
Abundant throughout the state in winter, the kestrel
can also be found breeding in the High
Plains and upper Rio Grande Valley.

FIELD NOTES Once ranging from Texas' coastal
scrublands to Arizona's open grasslands, the Aplomado
Falcon, *Falco femoralis* (inset), is endangered in
Texas. Since 1993, Laguna Atascosa National
Wildlife Refuge has been host to a reintroduction
program of captive-raised birds in the hopes of
one day reestablishing this handsome bird as a
trademark of the Southwest.

Year-round | Adult

KING RAIL

Rallus elegans L 15" (38 cm)

FIELD MARKS
Dark brown back feathers edged
in buff

Brown head with lighter cheeks
and buffy eyebrows

Flanks barred blackish and white

Long, slightly decurved bill

Behavior
Mainly terrestrial, prefers to swim short distances
instead of flying. Feeds in the open only at low tide on
plants, seeds, aquatic invertebrates, and other small
vertebrates. Population appears related to that of the
muskrat, which clears away enough marsh vegetation
to allow a foraging niche for the King Rail, though the
rail is able to compress its body laterally in order to
disappear into dense reeds. Call is a deep, evenly spaced
series of fewer than ten *kek-kek-kek* notes.

Habitat
Freshwater or brackish marshes and swamps, irrigation
ditches, and weedy lakes. Both male and female build
nest atop aquatic vegetation of marshes and lakes.

Local Sites
Commonly found in summer in marshes throughout
a large part of East Texas, tends primarily toward the
coast in winter. The marshy ponds of Anahuac
National Wildlife Refuge are good spots to listen for its
metronome-like call.

FIELD NOTES Even where common, the King Rail can be easily
overlooked, but not so easily overheard. Its grunted series of *kek*
notes is slower, deeper, and more evenly spaced than its similarly plumaged and similarly sized saltwater cousin, the Clapper
Rail, *Rallus longirostris*, which resides in coastal areas of Texas.

Year-round | Adult

AMERICAN COOT

Fulica americana L 15½" (39 cm)

FIELD MARKS
Blackish head; slate gray body

Small, reddish brown forehead
shield; reddish eyes on adult

Whitish bill with dark band at tip

Greenish legs with lobed toes

Juvenile paler with darker bill

Behavior
The distinctive toes of the American Coot are flexible
and lobed, permitting it to swim well in open water
and even to dive in pursuit of aquatic vegetation and
invertebrates. Lobed toes also enable the coot to run on
water, flapping its wings rapidly in order to gain the
momentum it needs to take flight. Forages in large
flocks, especially during the winter. Has a wide
vocabulary of grunts, quacks, and chatter.

Habitat
Nests in freshwater marshes or near lakes and ponds.
Winters in both fresh and salt water. The coot has also
adapted to human-altered habitats, including sewage
lagoons for foraging and suburban lawns for roosting.

Local Sites
The coot is a common and widespread year-round
resident in wetland habitats across Texas.

FIELD NOTES The slightly smaller Common
Moorhen, *Gallinula chloropus* (inset), inhabits many
of the same freshwater wetlands as the coot. It has a
bright red forehead shield which extends onto a red bill
tipped with yellow. The white line down
its side is another good field mark.

Year-round | Adult

WHOOPING CRANE

Grus americana L 52" (132 cm) W 87" (221 cm)

FIELD MARKS
White overall with bare, red skin on crown

Black wing tips show in flight

Blackish red moustachial stripe

Dull yellow bill; long, black legs

Juvenile reddish brown above

Behavior
The tallest bird in North America and one of the most endangered, forages on surface of water for fish, frogs, and crustaceans, and in fields for acorns, berries, and grain. Long neck is extended in flight, unlike herons. Roosts standing in shallow water, out of reach of most predators. Monogamous for life, silent courtship dance consists of leaps and bounds with head arched backwards, bill pointed skyward, legs stiff, and wings flapping. Call is a shrill, trumpeting *ker-loo ker-lee-loo*.

Habitat
Sparse wild population winters in marshes of Aransas National Wildlife Refuge on Gulf Coast; breeds in Wood Buffalo National Park in Alberta, Canada.

Local Sites
The best way to see one of these beautiful rarities is to hop on one of the commercial tour boats that regularly ply the marshes of Aransas Bay between mid-October and late April.

FIELD NOTES The only other native North American crane, the Sandhill Crane, *Grus canadensis* (inset), also has bare red skin on its crown and lores, but is smaller and gray overall. It can be found in large numbers every winter at Muleshoe National Wildlife Refuge.

Breeding | Adult

BLACK-BELLIED PLOVER

Pluvialis squatarola L 11½" (29 cm)

FIELD MARKS
Roundish head and body; large
eyes; short black bill; dark legs

Mottled gray with white underparts in winter and juveniles

Breeding male has frosted cap;
black and white spots on back
and wings; black face and breast

Behavior
Hunts in small, loose groups for invertebrates such as
mollusks, worms, shrimp, insects, and small crabs,
along with eggs and sometimes berries. Locates prey by
sight, runs across the ground, stops, then runs off
again. In this respect, a plover has a similar hunting
style to that of a thrush, such as an American Robin.
Long, pointed wings enable swift flight. Listen for the
Black-bellied Plover's drawn-out three-note whistle,
pee-oo-ee, the second note lower in pitch.

Habitat
This shorebird prefers sandy beaches, mudflats, and
salt marshes. Rarely found in interior regions. Breeds
on the Arctic tundra.

Local Sites
Though a common migrant throughout much of Texas
between March and April and between August and
November, the Black-bellied is abundant at any
number of sandy, coastal sites in winter.

FIELD NOTES During spring migration, look
for the Black-bellied's characteristic breeding
plumage (opposite). During winter, the Black-
bellied sheds its black-and-white feathers and
dons a drabber gray plumage (inset) to blend
into its sandy environs.

Year-round | Adult

KILLDEER

Charadrius vociferus L 10½" (27 cm)

FIELD MARKS

Gray-brown above; white neck and belly; two black breast bands

Black stripe on forehead and one extending back from black bill

Red-orange rump visible in flight

Red orbital ring

Behavior

Often seen running, then stopping on a dime with an inquisitive look, then suddenly jabbing at the ground with its bill. Feeds mainly on insects that live in short vegetation. May gather in loose flocks. The Killdeer's loud, piercing, eponymous call of *kill-dee* or its rising *dee-dee-dee* is often the signal for identifying these birds before sighting them. Listen also for a long, trilled *trrrrrrr* during courtship displays or when a nest is threatened by a predator.

Habitat

Although a type of plover—one of the shorebirds—the Killdeer prefers inland grassy regions, but also may be found on shores. Builds its nest on about any spot of open ground.

Local Sites

One of the most ubiquitous birds in Texas, the Killdeer can be found year-round in open areas across the state.

FIELD NOTES If its nest is threatened by an intruder, the Killdeer is known to feign a broken wing, limping to one side, dragging its wing, and spreading its tail in an attempt to lure the threat away from its young. Once the predator is far enough away from the nest, the instantly healed Killdeer takes flight.

Year-round | Adult

AMERICAN OYSTERCATCHER

Haematopus palliatus L 18½" (47 cm)

FIELD MARKS
Large, red-orange bill; pink legs

Black head and neck; dark brown back and tail

White underparts and wing stripe

Juvenile is scaly-looking above, with dark tip on bill

Behavior
Feeds in shallow water alone or in a flock. Uses its chisel-shaped bill to crack an opening in the shells of clams, oysters, and mussels; it then severs the shellfish's constrictor muscle and pries the shell open. Also probes sand and mud for worms and crabs. Courtship consists of calls coupled with ritualized flights of shallow, rapid wing beats and displays of side-by-side running or rotating in place. Calls are vocal and variable, including a piercing, repeated whistle; a loud, piping *queep*; and a single loud whistle.

Habitat
Coastal beaches, mudflats, and spoil islands. Nests in a scrape or bowl-shaped depression in sand or grass, or on gravel and shells piled above the tide line.

Local Sites
Residing along the entire Gulf Coast, oystercatchers are most common in the vicinity of Matagorda Bay. They almost never stray far from coastal waters.

FIELD NOTES American Oystercatchers are quite wary of humans and generally do not allow close approach. Keep an ear out though for their loud calls which are as distinctive as their bills.

Breeding | Adult male

AMERICAN AVOCET

Recurvirostra americana L 18" (46 cm)

FIELD MARKS
Rusty head and neck become
grayish in winter

Black and white back, white belly

Sharply upcurved bill, longer and
straighter in males

Long, bluish legs and feet

Behavior
This graceful wader feeds with a flock in shallow water
by walking in a loose line of sometimes 100 birds,
sweeping its slightly open bill in a scything motion just
below the water's surface, filtering in small organisms
such as aquatic larvae and small crustaceans. In deeper
water, may feed by tipping over, much like a dabbling
duck. Its bill is so sensitive that it will defend itself
solely with wings and feet. Call is a loud *wheet* or *pleeet*.

Habitat
Prefers coastal areas, shallow alkaline lakes, and briney
ponds for foraging. Nests on flat ground near water.

Local Sites
Avocets arrive on the Gulf Coast for winter in mid-
August, flocking by the hundreds, even thousands, to
Bolivar Flats near Anahuac National Wildlife Refuge.
They also breed on the High Plains.

FIELD NOTES The only other North American member of the family *Recurvirostridae*, the Black-
necked Stilt, *Himantopus mexicanus* (inset),
has exceptionally long, pinkish red legs,
which enable it to forage with its needle-
thin bill in waters deeper than most shore-
birds. Inhabiting much of the avocet's range in Texas, the stilt is
easily distinguished by its all-black back and its white cheeks.

Nonbreeding | Adult

GREATER YELLOWLEGS

Tringa melanoleuca L 14" (36 cm)

FIELD MARKS
Long, dark, slightly upturned bill;
long, bright yellow-orange legs

Head and neck streaked gray-
brown; white-speckled, gray-
brown back

White underparts slightly barred
gray-brown on flanks

Behavior
A forager of snails, crabs, and shrimp; also skims
surface of water for insects and larvae. Sprints short
distances in pursuit of small fish. Usually seen alone or
in small groups, this wary bird sounds an alarm when a
hawk or falcon approaches. Call is distinctive series of
three or more loud, repeated, descending *tew-tew-tew*
sounds, heard most often in flight.

Habitat
In winter, frequents a full range of wetlands, including
marshes, ponds, lakes, rivers, and reservoirs. Breeds
across the Canadian boreal zone.

Local Sites
Like its cousin, the Lesser Yellowlegs, the Greater is a
common migrant throughout Texas. In winter, both
species can be found at coastal sites such as Galveston
Island State Park and Laguna Atascosa
National Wildlife Refuge.

FIELD NOTES The Lesser Yellowlegs, *Tringa flavipes*
(inset), has a more restricted, coastal winter range in
Texas. Distinguished by its shorter, straighter
bill—about the length of its head—it is smaller in
stature and less wary in behavior. The Lesser's
call is higher and shorter too, consisting of one or two *tew* notes.

Breeding | Adult

WILLET

Catoptrophorus semipalmatus L 15" (38 cm)

FIELD MARKS
Large and plump; long gray legs

Breeding adult is heavily mottled
brownish gray above; white belly

Winter plumage pale gray above

In flight, shows black and white
wing pattern

Behavior
The Willet, like other shorebirds, wades in search of
prey, probing through mud with its long bill. Feeds
primarily on aquatic insects and their larvae. Flies low
to the ground, alternating rapid wing beats with short
glides. A male defending his breeding territory is quick
to scold, or even attack, intruders to its nest. Its breeding call of *pill-o-will-willet* is the origin of its name. It
may also be heard giving a *kip-kip-kip* alarm call.

Habitat
Common on beaches and coastal salt marshes. Nests on
sand in grassy vegetation.

Local Sites
Abundant year-round at sites all along the Gulf Coast,
nonresident populations can also be found inland during migration between late March and mid-May and
between mid-July and mid-September.

FIELD NOTES During courtship displays and in
flight (inset), the Willet will show its distinctive
black-and-white wing bands, one of its most
identifiable field marks. Keep an eye out as well
for the Willet's characteristic white rump.

Molting | Adult

SANDERLING

Calidris alba L 8" (20 cm)

FIELD MARKS
Pale gray above, white below

Bill and legs black

Prominent white stripe and black leading edge show on wing while in flight

Juveniles black-and-white above

Behavior
Feeds on sandy beaches, chasing retreating waves in order to snatch up newly exposed crustaceans and mollusks, then darting to avoid oncoming surf. Like many shorebirds, may be seen standing for a long time on one leg. Flies swiftly, aided by ample wing length and sharp, pointed wings. Flocks wheel and turn together in the air. Call is a sharp *kip*, often emitted in a series.

Habitat
Winters on sandy beaches of the United States and throughout most of the Southern Hemisphere. Migrates sometimes as many as 8,000 miles from breeding grounds in remote Arctic and subarctic.

Local Sites
A common sight on almost any sandy Texas beach in winter. Look for a Sanderling beginning to acquire a rusty wash on its head and back before departing for breeding grounds in late July.

FIELD NOTES The Dunlin, *Calidris alpina* (inset), is another small, pale winter inhabitant of Texas' sandy shorelines. It is slightly darker above and has a diffuse, dark gray breast band. Its bill is also longer and slightly decurved toward the tip.

Nonbreeding | Adult

LEAST SANDPIPER

Calidris minutilla L 6" (15 cm)

FIELD MARKS
Short, thin, slightly decurved bill
Gray-brown upperparts
Streaked gray-brown breast band
White belly and undertail coverts
Yellowish to greenish legs

Behavior
Forages for food with its short, spiky bill. Feeds on worms, insects, mollusks, small crabs, and fish, in muddy, sandy, or shallow water. Not wary of humans, it will investigate picnic sites on the beach. If flushed, flies off rapidly in a zigzag flight pattern. The Least Sandpiper's call is a high *kreee.*

Habitat
Common in coastal tidal regions and wetlands with exposed mud or sand. Flocks of up to 50 birds can appear on exposed mudflats both on the coast and inland. Breeds in Arctic regions.

Local Sites
The Least is perhaps the most common migrant shore-bird in Texas, most abundant in winter along the coast at any number of sites. Look for it in mudflats and marshes on the bay side of Texas' barrier islands.

FIELD NOTES The most diminutive of shorebirds collectively known as "peeps," the Least Sandpiper's yellow-green legs set it apart from the slightly larger Western Sandpiper, *Calidris mauri*, which has black legs. The Least's bill is also slightly shorter and its breast band more pronounced. These two peeps' winter range in Texas overlaps only near the coast.

Nonbreeding | Adult

LONG-BILLED DOWITCHER

Limnodromus scolopaceus L 11½" (29 cm)

FIELD MARKS

Long, straight, dark bill

Brownish gray above, paler below with strong barring on flanks

Pale eyebrow; yellow-green legs

Juvenile has rufous edges on back feathers

Behavior

A tactile feeder, hunts worms, insects, mollusks, small crabs, larvae, and fish by probing bottom mud with rapid jabbing motion of its bill, likened to a sewing machine. Will immerse head in water to probe shallows. While feeding, flocks emit a constant soft chatter, unlike closely related Short-billed Dowitcher, which generally remains silent while feeding. Call is a sharp, high-pitched *keek*, generally given in flight singly or in a rapid series.

Habitat

Prefers shallow freshwater ponds and marshes with muddy bottoms, generally in coastal areas.

Local Sites

A common migrant throughout the state, the Long-billed is most abundant on the coast during winter. Its fall migration tends to start in late July, a couple of weeks later than the Short-billed.

FIELD NOTES The closely related Short-billed Dowitcher, *Limnodromus griseus* (inset), is only slightly smaller and its bill is in fact not very noticeably shorter. The Short-billed is less vocal than its cousin, uttering a mellow *tu tu tu* call in flight, as opposed to the Long-billed's high-pitched *keek*. Both species have a V-shaped white patch extending up the back from the tail.

Breeding | Adult

LAUGHING GULL

Larus atricilla L 16½" (42 cm) W 40" (102 cm)

FIELD MARKS
Breeding adult has black hood; white underparts; slate gray wings with black outer primaries

White crescent marks above and below eyes; drooping red bill

In winter, gray wash on head, nape, and neck; black bill

Behavior

Forages for crabs, insects, decayed fish, garbage, and anything else it can get, sometimes plunging its head underwater or harassing beachgoers for popcorn or french fries. Large flocks can be observed feeding in coastal estuaries. Flocks often congregate around fishing boats, seeking scraps or discarded offal. Name comes from characteristic call, *ha-ha-ha-ha*, given when feeding or courting.

Habitat

Common and conspicuous at sandy beaches. Nests of grass and sticks are found in marshes or on sand.

Local Sites

Abundant on sandy beaches along the entire Gulf Coast, Laughing Gulls have also established small colonies inland at Falcon and Choke Canyon Reservoirs.

FIELD NOTES It takes three years for the Laughing Gull to attain full adult plumage. The juvenile is brown with a white throat and belly. By the first winter (inset), it still has brown wings, but its sides and back are gray. By the second winter it has lost all brown. Not until its third summer does it develop a black hood, the sign of a full breeding adult.

Nonbreeding | Adult

RING-BILLED GULL

Larus delawarensis L 17½" (45 cm) W 48" (122 cm)

FIELD MARKS
Yellow bill with black subterminal ring; pale eye with dark orbital ring

Pale gray upperparts; white underparts; yellowish legs; black primaries show white spots

Head streaked brown in winter

Behavior
This opportunistic feeder will scavenge for garbage, grains, dead fish, fruit, and marine invertebrates. A vocal gull, it calls, croaks, and cries incessantly, especially during feeding. The call consists of a series of laughing croaks that begins with a short, gruff note and falls into a series of *kheeyaahhh* sounds.

Habitat
More common along the coast, but also a regular visitor to most inland bodies of water, especially reservoirs in urban areas.

Local Sites
Abundant in winter throughout coastal regions, the Ring-billed Gull also frequents a multitude of parking lots and garbage dumps inland.

FIELD NOTES The Ring-billed Gull and its partner in crime, the Herring Gull, *Larus argentatus* (inset), are two of the more common winter gulls on the Texas shoreline. Very similar overall, the larger Herring has a red spot on its lower mandible, rather than a black ring, and has pinkish legs and feet. Both clever omnivores, they are known to use pavement to crack open clam shells dropped from 50 or 60 feet above.

Breeding | Adult

GULL-BILLED TERN

Sterna nilotica L 14" (36 cm) W 34" (86 cm)

FIELD MARKS

Black crown and nape, stout
black bill, black legs and feet

Pale gray above, white below

Tail not as forked as on other terns

Juvenile has pale head and
brownish bill

Behavior

Hunts insects, its main food source, over fields and
marshes in a direct flight aided by easy, graceful wing
beats, sometimes hovering over prey. Swoops down to
grab crabs, frogs, and spiders as well, but never plunge-
dives like most other terns. Nests in small colonies,
sometimes, though not usually, near the edge of other
terns' colonies. Adult's calls include a raspy, sharp *kay-
wack* and a guttural *za-za-za*; juvenile's a faint, high-
pitched *peep peep*.

Habitat

Prefers coastal grassy salt marshes abundant in insect
prey. Nests in shallow scrapes on sand or loose rocks in
small colonies.

Local Sites

The Gull-billed breeds locally along the entire Gulf
Coast in grassy coastal marshes such as those found at
Laguna Atascosa National Wildlife Refuge. Numbers
decrease in winter as some populations migrate toward
South America.

FIELD NOTES In the early 1900s, Gull-billed Terns were
endangered by decades of losing their eggs to restauranteurs
and their feathers to milliners. The species has never completely
recovered, and is now one of the least common tern species
resident on Texas' Gulf Coast.

Breeding | Adult

CASPIAN TERN

Sterna caspia L 21" (53 cm) W 50" (127 cm)

FIELD MARKS

Large, thick, red bill with dark tip

Pale gray above, white below

Breeding adult has black cap; winter adult's crown dusky

In flight, shows dark primary tips and forked tail

Behavior

Usually solitary, often hovers before plunge-diving for small fish, its main food source. Also swims gull-like and feeds from the water's surface. The largest tern in the world, the Caspian is quite predatory by nature, frequently stealing catches from other gulls and terns, and feeding on their eggs and chicks. Adult's calls include a harsh *kowk* and *ca-arr*. Juvenile call is high, thin whistled *whee-you*.

Habitat

Locally common and widespread on coastlines throughout the world, small colonies nest together on beaches or in wetlands.

Local Sites

A common year-round resident on the Texas Gulf Coast, the Caspian Tern can be found on most any sandy beach. In winter, it can be found in a group of other gulls and terns.

FIELD NOTES Another year-round resident of the Texas Gulf Coast is the Royal Tern, *Sterna maxima* (inset: juvenile, left; nonbreeding, right). The second largest tern of North America, the Royal is smaller and sleeker than its cousin, with a more deeply forked tail and a yellow-orange bill.

Molting | Adult

FORSTER'S TERN

Sterna forsteri **L** 14½" (37 cm)

FIELD MARKS
Pale gray above; white below

Full black cap on breeding adult;
only around eye in fall and winter

Orange-red bill with dark tip while
breeding; all dark in winter

Long, deeply forked gray tail

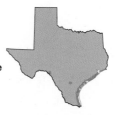

Behavior
When feeding, the Forster's flies back and forth over
the water, then plunge-dives to capture small fish. May
also forage on insects, grabbing them in the air or from
the water's surface. Often feeds and flocks with other
species of tern. Gives a one-note call, a hoarse,
descending *kyarr,* while feeding over water or during
breeding season. Also emits a piercing *kit-kit-kit* cry.

Habitat
Winters mainly along coastlines, but also inhabits
inland marshes and lakes where abundant fish and
insects may be found. Nests in loose colonies in salt
marshes atop a platform of grass, or in sand or mud.

Local Sites
A year-round resident along Texas' coastline, the
Forster's is also a common migrant throughout the
entire state. Look for it in summer among the grasses
of Texas' coastal salt marshes.

FIELD NOTES The endangered Least Tern,
Sterna antillarum (inset), nests
on sandy beaches all along the
Texas coast. Considerably smaller than the
Forster's Tern, it is the smallest tern to occur in North
America. It has a yellow bill and legs, a white forehead, and
shows a black wedge on its outer primaries in flight.

Breeding | Adult

BLACK SKIMMER

Rynchops niger L 18" (46 cm) W 44" (112 cm)

FIELD MARKS
Long, red, black-tipped bill with
lower mandible longer than upper

Black back and crown; white face
and underparts; red legs

Winter adults show white collar

Female distinctly smaller

Behavior
Uses long, pointed wings to glide low over water while
dropping its lower mandible to skim the surface for
small fish. Once its bill touches a fish, the maxilla, or
upper bill, snaps down to catch prey. Breeds in colonies
on beaches, often sharing a site with tern species to take
advantage of their aggressive defensive tactics. Makes a
yelping bark in nesting colonies or in response to a
threat. Pairs sometimes sing a *kow-kow* call together.

Habitat
Prefers sheltered bays, estuaries, coastal marshes, and
sometimes inland lakes. Nests very locally in large
colonies on barrier islands and salt marshes.

Local Sites
Though currently being crowded out of nesting
grounds by increased development, the Black Skimmer
can still be found skimming the shorelines of Galveston
Island State Park.

FIELD NOTES The Black Skimmer has a unique bill: As a feeding
adaptation, the lower mandible is considerably longer than the
upper. It also has an adaptive pupil, able to contract to a narrow,
vertical slit. This capability is thought to protect the eye from
bright sunlight glaring off the water's surface.

Year-round | Adult

ROCK PIGEON

Columba livia L 12½" (32 cm)

FIELD MARKS
Highly variable in its multicolored
hues, with head and neck usually
darker than back

White cere, dark bill, pink legs

Iridescent feathers on neck reflect
green, bronze, and purple

Behavior
Feeds during the day on grain, seeds, fruit, or refuse in
cities and suburbs, parks, and fields; a frequent visitor
to farms and backyard feeding stations as well. As it
forages, the Rock Pigeon moves with a short-stepped,
"pigeon-toed" gait while its head bobs back and forth.
Courtship display consists of the male puffing out neck
feathers, fanning his tail, and turning in circles while
cooing; results in a pairing that could last for life.
Characterized by soft *coo-cuk-cuk-cuk-cooo* call.

Habitat
Anywhere near human habitation. Nests and roosts
primarily on high window ledges, on bridges, and in
barns. Builds nest of stiff twigs, sticks, and leaves.

Local Sites
Introduced from Europe by settlers in the 1600s, now
widespread and abundant throughout most developed
regions of North America.

FIELD NOTES The Eurasian Collared-
Dove, *Streptopelia decaocto* (inset),
was also introduced into North America from
Europe. Starting from the Bahama Islands in 1974,
it reached Texas by 1995 and is now fairly common
in urban areas throughout the state.

Year-round | Adult

WHITE-WINGED DOVE

Zenaida asiatica L 11½" (29 cm)

FIELD MARKS
Brownish gray overall with
conspicuous white wing patches

Black mark on sides of neck

Bare blue skin surrounds orange-
red eyes

Rounded tail with white corners

Behavior
A desert inhabitant, will fly more than 20 miles in
order to reach a source of water, whether a natural
source, such as a stream or cactus, or a man-made
source, such as a reservoir, canal, or cattle trough. Eats
seeds, grain, and fruit. In-flight courtship display
consists of male clapping his wings as he rises, then
descending on stiff wings. Call is a low-pitched, drawn-
out *who-cooks-for-you*, reminiscent of Barred Owl.

Habitat
Historically a bird of deserts and brushlands, the
White-winged Dove is currently increasing in urban
areas with scattered trees. Nests, sometimes in colonies,
in shrubs, mesquite, cacti, or low in trees.

Local Sites
Currently expanding its range throughout much of
Texas, the White-winged can be found in large num-
bers year-round in and around the city of San Antonio.

FIELD NOTES The widespread and abundant Mourning
Dove, *Zenaida macroura* (inset), can be found in most
any habitat of North America. It is distinguished from
the White-winged by its long, pointed tail,
black spotting on its upperwings, and its
lack of wing bars.

Year-round | Adult

INCA DOVE

Columbina inca L 8¼" (21 cm)

FIELD MARKS
Gray-buff body, paler on face

Dark edges on feathers create
conspicuously scalloped pattern

Long, square-ended tail edged
in white

Shows chestnut primaries in flight

Behavior
Forages on the ground for seeds and grain, often in the
company of other small doves or even of chickens on
ranchlands. Ascends to perch to roost, huddled into a
makeshift pyramid with other Inca Doves during
colder months. A common visitor to feeders and birdbaths within its range. Male puffs out chest feathers
during courtship strut. Call is a mellow *coo-coo*,
repeated twice.

Habitat
Common near human habitation in semiarid regions.
Female builds platform nest of twigs fairly low to
ground in tree or shrub.

Local Sites
The Inca Dove is a common resident throughout the
southern two-thirds of Texas. Currently expanding its
range northward and eastward, it has even been spotted
in Kansas and Arkansas.

FIELD NOTES Sharing the Inca's scale-like
scalloping on its head and breast, the
Common Ground-Dove, *Columbina passe-*
rina (inset), a resident of Texas' southern
brush country and coastal prairies, is distinguished by its short,
dark tail and its diminutive size; it is barely larger than a sparrow.

Year-round | Adult

YELLOW-BILLED CUCKOO

Coccyzus americanus L 12" (31 cm)

FIELD MARKS

Gray-brown above, white below

Decurved bill with dark upper mandible and yellow lower

Long tail patterned underneath in bold black and white

Yellow orbital ring

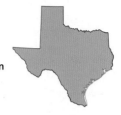

Behavior

This shy species slips quietly through woodlands, combing the vegetation for caterpillars, frogs, lizards, cicadas, and other insects. Recognized as an important predator of harmful caterpillars. During courtship, male will climb on female's shoulders to feed her from above. Unique song sounds hollow and wooden, a rapid staccato *kuk-kuk-kuk* that usually descends to a *kakakowlp-kowlp* ending; it is heard often in the spring and summer.

Habitat

Common in dense canopies of woods, orchards, and streamside groves. Also inhabits tangles of swamp edges. Nests lined with grasses and moss located on horizontal tree limbs. Winters in South America.

Local Sites

A common migrant and summer resident throughout Texas. Look for the Yellow-billed Cuckoo in dense woodland thickets between April and October.

FIELD NOTES A stealthy forager, the Yellow-billed Cuckoo is often more common than it appears. Listen for its distinctive song, often emitted just before a storm, a habit that has earned it the nickname, the "rain crow."

Year-round | Adult

GREATER ROADRUNNER

Geococcyx californianus L 23" (58 cm)

FIELD MARKS
Streaked brown and white overall

Long tail edged in white

Long, heavy bill with hooked tip

Conspicuous, bushy crest

Short, rounded wings show a
white crescent in flight

Behavior
A largely terrestrial bird, the roadrunner generally runs
rather than flies, but will glide low to the ground to
gain a perch on a fence post or rock. An aggressive
feeder, it eats insects, lizards, snakes, rodents, and small
birds, sometimes raiding a nest for young hatchlings.
Pairs may even take prey as formidable as a rattlesnake.
Song is a slow low-pitched dovelike cooing, descending
in pitch. It is most often heard during nesting season.

Habitat
Inhabits dry, open areas such as scrub desert, mesquite
groves, and grassland. Less common in chaparral and
open woodland. Nests in shrubs, trees, or cacti.

Local Sites
A year-round resident throughout Texas, the roadrunner can even be found in eastern pine woods,
though it is much more common in
southwestern scrub desert.

FIELD NOTES Another unusual member of the
family *Cuculidae* and a Texas specialty, the
Groove-billed Ani, *Crotophaga sulcirostris* (inset),
acts almost as comically as it looks. When landing,
it almost seems as if it could fall off its perch as its
long tail flips up over its head. It is a regular
breeder in the lower Rio Grande Valley.

Year-round | Adult rufous morph

EASTERN SCREECH-OWL

Megascops asio L 8½" (22 cm)

FIELD MARKS
Small yellow eyes and pale tip on
yellow-green bill

Underparts marked by vertical
streaks crossed by dark bars

Ear tufts prominent if raised

Round, flattened facial disk

Behavior
Nocturnal; uses exceptional vision and hearing to hunt
for mice, voles, shrews, and insects. If approached while
roosting during the day, it will stretch its body, erect its
ear tufts, and shut its eyes to blend into its background.
Rufous, gray, and brown morphs exist, with the rufous
morph dominant in eastern Texas, the gray morph in
central and southern Texas. Emits a series of quavering
whistles, descending in pitch, or a long, one-pitch trill,
most often heard in winter and spring.

Habitat
Common in a wide variety of habitats including wood-
lots, forests, swamps, orchards, parks, and suburban
gardens. Nests in trees about 10 to 30 feet up.

Local Sites
A tremulous whistle will sometimes lure the Screech-
Owl out of the dense cover of woodlands throughout
East Texas. Its call is rather easy to imitate and the owl
responds readily.

FIELD NOTES The Eastern Screech-Owl's counterpart, the Western Screech-Owl, *Megascops kenni-
cottii* (inset), occurs in Texas only in its gray morph.
It is best differentiated by its range, occuring for the
most part west of the Pecos River, and its voice, a
series of short whistles, accelerating in tempo.

Year-round | Adult

GREAT HORNED OWL

Bubo virginianus L 22" (56 cm)

FIELD MARKS
Mottled brownish gray above, densely barred below

Long ear tufts (or "horns")

Rust-colored facial disks

Yellow eyes; white chin and throat; buff-colored underwings

Behavior
Chiefly nocturnal. Feeds on a variety of animals including cats, skunks, porcupines, birds, snakes, grouse, and frogs; watches from high perch, then swoops down on prey. One of the earliest birds to nest, beginning in January or February, possibly to take advantage of winter-stressed prey. Call is a series of three to eight loud, deep hoots, the second and third often short and rapid.

Habitat
The most widespread owl in North America, the Great Horned Owl can be found in a wide variety of habitats including forests, cities, and farmlands. Reuses abandoned nests of other large birds.

Local Sites
A year-round resident across Texas, the Great Horned is common in its paler form west of the Pecos River, where it is a dominant avian predator.

FIELD NOTES Only slightly smaller than the Great Horned, the Barred Owl, *Strix varia* (inset), inhabits a variety of woodlands in East Texas. Its loud rhythmic call, *who-cooks-for-you*, *who-cooks-for-you-all*, is much more likely to be heard during the day than most owls' calls.

Year-round | Adult

BURROWING OWL

Athene cunicularia L 9½" (24 cm)

FIELD MARKS
Brown above with white spotting
on back, white streaks on crown

White below with brown bars

Large, yellow eyes topped by
broad white eyebrow

Long legs

Behavior
A terrestrial owl, forages primarily at night, dawn, and
dusk on insects and small mammals such as mice.
Flight is low and undulating; can hover like a kestrel.
Regularly perches on the ground or on low posts
during the day next to its burrow. Nests in single pairs
or small colonies often in prairie dog towns, enlarging
and reshaping the small mammals' already existing
burrows by kicking dirt out backwards. Calls include a
soft *co-coooo* and a chattering series of *chack* notes.

Habitat
Open grasslands and prairies. Nests in abandoned
burrows of prairie dogs, ground squirrels, or gophers.

Local Sites
Though declining throughout its North American
range, the Burrowing Owl can still be found breeding
in the Panhandle and West Texas. Look for them in the
prairie dog town near the headquarters of Muleshoe
National Wildlife Refuge.

FIELD NOTES If disturbed at the nest, both parent and hatchling
Burrowing Owls often give alarm call of a rapid chatter, which
imitates the sound of a rattlesnake's rattle.

Year-round | Adult

COMMON PAURAQUE

Nyctidromus albicollis L 11" (28 cm)

FIELD MARKS

Upperparts patterned in black, buff, and gray

Buff underparts barred with black

Chestnut ear patches

In flight, shows long, rounded tail and broad, pale band on wings

Behavior

Roosts during the day on the ground, where it blends in with leaf litter so well that it is virtually unnoticeable until flushed, when it gives soft *kwup* call. Sits on ground at night, darting up to catch flying insects. Rarely flies more than ten feet off the ground, sometimes snatching insects attracted to headlights of a car. Loud song begins with one or more low *pur* notes, followed by a higher, descending *wheeer*. It is most often heard on moonlit nights.

Habitat

Woodland clearings and brushy scrublands. Nests on the ground using no nesting materials.

Local Sites

The Common Pauraque's range in North America is limited to the brush country of South Texas. Listen for them year-round at Laguna Atascosa National Wildlife Refuge.

FIELD NOTES The far more widespread Common Nighthawk, *Chordeiles minor* (inset), is another of Texas's goatsuckers, so named for the old legend that these birds would enter barns at night to suckle from goats. A summer resident in much of Texas, the nighthawk is told apart from the pauraque in flight by its notched tail and long, pointed wings.

Year-round | Adult

CHIMNEY SWIFT

Chaetura pelagica L 5¼" (13 cm)

FIELD MARKS
Short, cigar-shaped body

Long, pointed, narrow wings

Dark plumage, sooty gray overall

Short, stubby tail

Blackish gray bill, legs, feet

Behavior
Soars with long wings at great speeds, often in a circle, swooping to catch ants, termites, and spiders while in flight. Look for large groups of Chimney Swifts circling above rooftops at dusk before dropping into chimneys to roost. During aerial courtship, the suitor raises its wings into a sharp V. Its call is high-pitched chattering.

Habitat
Builds cup-shaped nests of small twigs glued together with dried saliva in chimneys, under eaves of abandoned barns, and in hollow trees. Roosts in chimneys and steeples. Otherwise seen soaring over forested, open, or urban sites. Winters as far south as Peru.

Local Sites
Chimney Swifts can be seen best in summer at dusk, circling in large flocks and at great speeds over cities and towns from Corpus Christi north.

FIELD NOTES The Chimney Swift once confined its nests to tree hollows and other natural sites. Over the centuries, it has adapted so well to artificial nesting sites, such as chimneys, air shafts, vertical pipes, barns, and silos, that the species' numbers have increased dramatically. It is the only swift seen regularly in eastern and southern Texas.

Year-round | Adult

BUFF-BELLIED HUMMINGBIRD

Amazilia yucatanensis L 4¼" (11 cm)

FIELD MARKS

Metallic green head, throat, upper breast, and upperparts

Buff-colored lower breast, belly

Metallic chestnut tail

Black tip on decurved pinkish red bill, which is brighter on male

Behavior

Hovers at flowers to sip nectar, often visiting gardens and feeders. Sometimes takes insects in flight. Female builds nest of plant fibers, spider webs, and pieces of bark, then covers it in flower petals and lichen. Calls include a sharp, high-pitched *sik* when driving off intruders to territory, and a squeaky *chip* when perched, often repeated two to four times.

Habitat

This tropical species reaches its northern limit in the open oak woods, shrubby areas, and suburban gardens of southern Texas. Nests in fork of shrub or small tree.

Local Sites

Largely nonmigratory, the Buff-bellied Hummingbird can be found year-round in the southern tip of Texas near the lower Rio Grande Valley. Santa Ana National Wildlife Refuge or Sabal Palm Audubon Center and Sanctuary near Brownsville are two places to try.

FIELD NOTES Though most Buff-bellied Hummingbirds retreat south after breeding, some undertake a sort of reverse migration, breeding on the central Texas coast and migrating in the fall as far east as western Florida. In this way, they are expanding their range northward and inland.

Year-round | Adult male

Archilochus colubris L 3¾" (10 cm)

FIELD MARKS
Metallic green above

Adult male has brilliant red gorget,
black chin, whitish underparts,
dusky green sides

Female lacks gorget, has whitish
throat and underparts, buffy wash
on sides

Behavior

Probes flowers and hummingbird feeders for nectar by
hovering virtually still in midair. Also feeds on small
spiders and insects. When nectar is scarce, the Ruby-
throated is known to drink sap from wells made in tree
trunks by sapsuckers. In spring, male Ruby-throateds
arrive in breeding territory before females and engage
in jousts to claim prime territory. In addition to the
hum generated by its rapidly beating wings, this bird
emits soft *tchiv* notes.

Habitat

Found in gardens and woodland edges throughout
most of the eastern United States. Female builds nest
on small, downsloping tree limbs.

Local Sites

The Ruby-throated is a common summer resident of
East Texas, west to the Edwards Plateau.

FIELD NOTES Where the Ruby-throated's range in
Texas reaches its western limit, there begins the
range of the similarly plumaged Black-chinned
Hummingbird, *Archilochus alexandri* (inset: male). The
male's gorget is violet in good light as opposed to red, and the
female has dusky gray flanks instead of buff.

Year-round | Adult Male

RINGED KINGFISHER

Ceryle torquata L 16" (41 cm)

FIELD MARKS
Blue-gray head with short, shaggy crest; blue-gray upperparts

Male's breast and belly rufous, underwings white; female's breast blue-gray bordered in white, rufous belly and underwings

Long, heavy, dark bill

Behavior
Generally solitary and vocal, dives headfirst for fish from a waterside perch or after hovering above in order to line up on its target. Also takes frogs and reptiles at times. Pairs are monogamous, and both parents help dig nesting burrow, and incubate and feed young. Calls include a loud, harsh, repeating rattle, *ke ke ke*, and a single *chack* note, given primarily in flight.

Habitat
Found along large rivers, lakes, and lagoons. Prefers areas that are partially wooded. Raises young in burrows dug out of the bank of a river.

Local Sites
Look for all three Texas kingfishers, including the stealthy and diminutive Green Kingfisher, *Chloroceryle americana*, along the lower Rio Grande Valley, at sites like Bentsen-Rio Grande Valley State Park and Falcon Reservoir.

FIELD NOTES The closely related Belted Kingfisher, *Ceryle alcyon* (inset: male), shares essentially the same behavioral characteristics as its slightly larger cousin, the Ringed Kingfisher. The Belted is far more widespread and abundant though, able to adapt to nearly any spot of water in North America. Note the male's largely white underparts and the female's chestnut belly band and flanks.

Year-round | Adult male

GOLDEN-FRONTED WOODPECKER

Melanerpes aurifrons L 9¾" (25 cm)

FIELD MARKS
Golden-orange on nape and
above bill; male has small red cap

Black-and-white barred back;
whitish below with yellowish tinge

White rump, unbarred black tail

Juvenile has streaked breast

Behavior

Usually solitary or in a pair, forages low on trees and on
ground for insects, spiders, berries, nuts, acorns, and
grain. Keeps store of food for winter in bark crevices.
Monogamous pair works together for over a week to
drill a nest cavity more than a foot deep into the trunk
of a dead mesquite tree, a fence post, or a utility pole.
Often uses same nesting site year after year. Parents also
share in incubation and feeding of young. Calls include
a rolling *churr-churr* and a cackling *kek-kek-kek*.

Habitat

Inhabits dry woodlands, mesquite brushlands, and
suburbs with a suitable amount of trees or utility poles.

Local Sites

Find Golden-fronteds in sites such as Pedernales Falls
State Park and Lost Maples State Natural Area, both
in Texas' Hill Country.

FIELD NOTES An eastern counterpart, the
Red-bellied Woodpecker, *Melanerpes caroli-
nus* (inset: female, left; male, right), essentially
takes up residence in Texas where the Golden-
fronted leaves off at the eastern edge of the
Edwards Plateau. It has a red nape, and a red
crown on the male, as well as a barred tail.

Year-round | Adult male

LADDER-BACKED WOODPECKER

Picoides scalaris L 7¼" (18 cm)

FIELD MARKS
Black-and-white barred back;
grayish below with black spots

Face is marked by white cheek,
outlined in black

Crown red on male, black on
female; both have black forehead

Behavior
Male and female split into microhabitats, with male
foraging lower to ground, primarily for ants; female
forages higher up in vegetation for other insects. Both
eat the fruit of cacti. Has uncanny ability to locate
stores of beetle larvae hidden beneath the bark of small
trees. Known also to frequent birdbaths and feeders.
Call used by male and female while foraging is a crisp,
high-pitched *pik*.

Habitat
Found in arid and semiarid brushlands, as well as in
mesquite and cactus country. Excavates precise, circular
nesting hole in dead limbs of small trees, in large cacti,
in yucca and agave plants, or in fence posts.

Local Sites
The common small woodpecker of southwestern Texas,
the Ladder-backed can be found in parks and reserves
from Big Bend to Muleshoe to Laguna Atascosa
National Wildlife Refuge.

FIELD NOTES The bone and muscle structure of a woodpecker's
head is an effective shock absorber; a necessary adaptation for
a bird that spends its time drilling into hard wood. Similarly, a stiff
tail and sharp claws help it to maintain an upright position
against a tree trunk for long stretches.

Year-round | Adult female

DOWNY WOODPECKER

Picoides pubescens L 6¾" (17 cm)

FIELD MARKS
Black cap, ear patch, malar stripe;
black wings with white spotting

Block of white on back

White tuft in front of eyes;
white underparts

Red occipital patch on male only

Behavior
The smallest woodpecker in North America, the
Downy forages mainly on insects, larvae, and eggs.
Readily visits backyard feeders for sunflower seeds and
suet. Will also consume poison ivy berries. Small size
enables it to forage on smaller, thinner limbs. Both
male and female stake territorial claims with their
drumming. Call is a high-pitched but soft *pik*.

Habitat
Common in suburbs, parks, and orchards, as well as
forests and woodlands. Nests in cavities of dead trees.

Local Sites
Both Downy and Hairy Woodpeckers tend to the
eastern third of Texas, where they can be found
throughout Sam Houston National Forest, or even at
backyard feeding stations.

FIELD NOTES The larger and less common Hairy
Woodpecker, *Picoides villosus* (inset), is similarly
marked but has a bill as long as its head and a
sharper, louder, lower-pitched call. It also tends to
stay on tree trunks or larger limbs than the Downy.
Note as well the all-white outer tail feathers of the
Hairy Woodpecker; the Downy's outer tail feathers
are often barred or spotted black.

Year-round | Adult female "Yellow-shafted"

NORTHERN FLICKER

Colaptes auratus L 12½" (32 cm)

FIELD MARKS
Yellowish underwing, white rump

Brown, barred back; cream
underparts with black spotting;
black crescent bib

Gray crown, tan face, red
crescent on nape, and, on male,
black moustachial stripe

Behavior
Feeds mostly on the ground, foraging primarily for
ants. A cavity-nesting bird, the flicker will drill into
wooden surfaces, including utility poles and houses.
Bows to its partner before engaging in a courtship
dance of exaggerated wing and tail movements. Call is
a long, loud series of *wick-er*, *wick-er* during breeding
season, or a single, loud *klee-yer* heard year-round.

Habitat
Prefers open woodlands and suburban areas with
sizeable living and dead trees. An insectivore, the
Northern Flicker is at least partially migratory,
traveling in the winter in pursuit of food.

Local Sites
A winter resident of Texas, the flicker is most common
in towns and cities in the northern half of the state.

FIELD NOTES Two distinct groups make up the Northern Flicker
species. The "Yellow-shafted" Flicker (described above) can be
found east from the central High Plains and eastern Edwards
Plateau. The "Red-shafted," found predominantly in the western
two-thirds of Texas, lacks the Yellow-shafted's red nape
crescent, shows red-orange wing linings, and the male has a red
moustachial stripe. Intergrades occur where ranges overlap.

EASTERN PHOEBE

Sayornis phoebe L 7" (18 cm)

FIELD MARKS
Brownish gray above, darkest on
head, wings, and tail; dark bill

Underparts mostly white with pale
olive wash on sides and breast

Fresh fall birds washed with
yellow on belly

Behavior
The Eastern Phoebe flicks its tail constantly when
perched, looking for flying insects to chase and snare in
midair. Also easts small fish, berries, and fruit. It is
among the first birds to migrate each spring. Its
distinctive eponymous song is a harsh, emphatic *fee-be*,
accented on the first syllable; often repeated when male
is attempting to lure a mate. Call is a sharp *chip*.

Habitat
Common in woodlands, farmlands, and suburbs. Often
builds delicate cup-like nest under bridges, in eaves,
and in rafters, usually near running water.

Local Sites
A common migrant throughout the state, the Eastern
Phoebe breeds in Texas's northern and central regions
and is especially abundant in winter along the coast.

FIELD NOTES The Say's Phoebe, *Sayornis
saya* (inset), largely replaces the Eastern
Phoebe where its range drops off in the western
High Plains and at the Pecos River. It has in
common with the Eastern Phoebe brownish gray
upperparts, but is distinctive in its tawny buff
belly and undertail coverts. Not as tied to
watery locales, it inhabits Texas's arid southwest.

Year-round | Adult male

VERMILION FLYCATCHER

Pyrocephalus rubinus L 6" (15 cm)

FIELD MARKS
Male has strikingly red crown, face, and underparts; blackish brown mask and upperparts

Female has grayish brown upperparts; white breast with dusky streaking; pinkish belly

Short black tail

Behavior
Generally seen alone or in a pair, perches on low branch to scan for prey, then darts after flying insects and snags them on the wing. Also pounces on prey on the ground from perch. Like a phoebe, pumps and spreads its tail continuously while perched. Call is a sharp, thin *pseep*.

Habitat
Found near sources of water in arid and semiarid regions, such as streamside shrubs, small wooded ponds, and man-made irrigation zones. Female builds nest of sticks, grass, weeds, and feathers in fork of tree.

Local Sites
This fairly approachable species can be found at ponds and open woodlands in summer in Big Bend National Park, Pedernales Falls State Park, or other nearby sites.

FIELD NOTES The female Vermilion Flycatcher (inset) sits witness to the male's charming aerial courtship display. As the male circles high into the air using methodical, exaggerated wing beats, he sings a soft, sputtering *pit-a-see pit-a-see*. Once at the height of his climb, he hovers, crown feathers erect, breast puffed out, and tail spread, and sings a rapid, high-pitched trill before descending back down to a perch beside his potential mate.

Year-round | Adult

GREAT KISKADEE

Pitangus sulphuratus L 9¾" (25 cm)

FIELD MARKS
Black-and-white striped head with
yellow crown patch often hidden

Bright yellow chest and belly

Brown above with reddish brown
wings and tail

White cheeks, chin, and throat

Behavior
By itself or in a pair, perches near water until it spots
prey, then dives in to snag fish and tadpoles. Also
catches flying insects, as well as frogs, lizards, baby
birds, even mice. Resorts to fruit and berries when live
prey is unavailable. Aggressively defends territory even
against larger birds. Loud and conspicuous, listen for
its slow, deliberate *kis-ka-dee*. Also emits a loud *cree-ah*
and a squealed *whee*.

Habitat
Found primarily in dense woodlands near water,
especially riparian habitats. Nests in dense tree or
shrub with grass, bark, and other plant material.

Local Sites
A year-round resident of the lower Rio Grande Valley.
Look for the kiskadee sunning itself in sites like Santa
Ana National Wildlife Refuge or Bentsen-Rio Grande
Valley State Park.

FIELD NOTES Though the kiskadee prefers to remain largely concealed within thick vegetation, its location is almost invariably
betrayed by its persistent, raucous chatter. A loud self-
proclaiming *kis-ka-dee* call from one bird will often elicit a
response from another one nearby.

Year-round | Adult

COUCH'S KINGBIRD

Tyrannus couchii **L 9¼" (24 cm)**

FIELD MARKS
Bright yellow underparts

Greenish gray back; brownish
wings and tail

Gray face and nape; whitish throat

Dark gray ear patch

Slightly notched tail

Behavior
Often in a pair or small group, forages by hovering over
vegetation or ground to pick insects, berries, and fruit.
Also perches to scan for prey, which it snatches on the
wing. Like other flycatchers, the Couch's is highly
territorial and will attack intruders. Distinctive calls
include a shrill, buzzy, rolling *breeer*, and a high sharp
kip, given once or repeated. Listen as well for a series of
high, thin whistles, sung mostly in early morning.

Habitat
Found in dense groves and shrubs with nearby open
areas, often along river valleys or coastlines. Nests on
tree limb with twigs, leaves, moss, and weeds.

Local Sites
The kingbird most likely to be found in the lower Rio
Grande Valley. Look for the Couch's Kingbird year-
round at Laguna Atascosa National Wildlife Refuge.

FIELD NOTES The primary breeding kingbird
along the entire rest of the Rio Grande Valley
and throughout much of Texas is the Western
Kingbird, *Tyrannus verticalis* (inset). Common
and widespread, it has adapted impressively to
the habits of man. It can be distinguished
from the Couch's by its squared-off black
tail, which is edged in white, and its ashy gray back.

Year-round | Adult

SCISSOR-TAILED FLYCATCHER

Tyrannus forficatus L 13" (33 cm)

FIELD MARKS
Extremely long, deeply forked
black-and-white tail

Pale gray head and back; dark
brown wings with white edges

Whitish breast; salmon-pink belly,
flanks, and underwings

Behavior
Scans for prey of bees, wasps, and other flying insects
from perch, then darts to catch them in midair. Also
scans ground for grasshoppers, crickets, and beetles
from low perch. Able to sit motionless, usually by itself,
for hours on end. Migrates in large, spectacular flocks
of hundreds of birds. Pugnaciously defends its territory
from the likes of crows and even hawks. Calls include a
sharp *kew*, a low *pik*, and a doubled *ka-lup*.

Habitat
Prefers prairies, savannas, and open country with scattered trees and bushes. Nests in fork of tree or often in
a man-made structure such as a utility pole. Winters in
southern Mexico and Central America.

Local Sites
Scissor-tailed Flycatchers begin arriving in Texas in late
February and can be found in open areas throughout
the eastern portions of the state until November.

FIELD NOTES As handsome as this bird may look when perched,
it is in its aerial acrobatics that it truly amazes. During courtship,
the male rises on fluttering wings to about a hundred feet, then
freewheels down in a zigzag pattern, stops up short, and com-
pletes two backward loops with its long tail trailing behind.

Year-round | Adult

WHITE-EYED VIREO

Vireo griseus L 5" (13 cm)

FIELD MARKS
Grayish olive above

White neck and belly; pale yellow
sides and flanks

Yellow spectacles; distinctive
white iris visible at close range

Two whitish wing bars

Behavior
Usually seen by itself. Its thick, blunt, slightly hooked
bill is used for catching flies and picking fruits and
berries. Known to sing into the heat of summer, the
White-eyed Vireo is characterized by a loud, grating,
jumbled, five- to seven-note call, usually beginning and
ending with a sharp *chick*. The notes run together, the
middle portion seeming to mimic other birds' songs.
Regional and individual variations abound, but the
standard, generic sequence is *quick-with-the-beer-check!*

Habitat
Prefers to conceal itself close to the ground in dense
thickets, brushy tangles, and forest overgrowth. Nests
close to the ground in shrub or small tree.

Local Sites
Most numerous in summer. Look for
the White-eyed Vireo east of the
Edwards Plateau.

FIELD NOTES The Red-eyed Vireo,
Vireo olivaceus, gets its name from
the adult of the species (inset, left). The
immature (inset, right), has a brown iris. In all ages, its
lack of wing bars and white eyebrow bordered in black
distinguish it readily from the more common White-eyed.

Year-round | Adult male

BLACK-CAPPED VIREO

Vireo atricapillus L 4½" (11 cm)

FIELD MARKS

Male's glossy black cap contrasts
with broken white spectacles

Female's head bluish gray

Olive above; white below; yellow
flanks, underwings, and wing bars

Behavior

This endangered species is quite difficult to see not just
due to its dwindling numbers, but due to its secretive
behavior. Usually by itself, it remains low in deep cover
of oak scrub and thickets, foraging actively for insects,
caterpillars, spiders, and larvae, as well as small fruit
and berries. Song is given persistently, even during
midday heat, a hurried string of varied, twittering two-
or three-note phrases. *Ji-dit* call is similar to Ruby-
crowned Kinglet's.

Habitat

Scrub and dense thicket of shin oak and other shrubs,
with nearby open spaces that allow a good amount of
direct sunlight. Nest suspended from fork of tree or
shrub close to ground. Winters in western Mexico.

Local Sites

The Black-capped still breeds locally in the Texas Hill
Country at sites like Balcones Canyonlands National
Wildlife Refuge and Kickapoo Cavern State Park.

FIELD NOTES Brood parasitism by the Brown-headed Cowbird is
a major factor in the Black-capped's endangered status, with
studies concluding that up to 90 percent of nests on the
Edwards Plateau are affected. Overbrowsing by livestock and
increased urbanization also threaten the bird's fragile ecosystem.

Year-round | Adult

GREEN JAY

Cyanocorax yncas L 10½" (27 cm)

FIELD MARKS
Pale green above; yellowish green
below; blue-green tail with yellow
outer tail feathers

Blue crown, nape, and cheek
mark contrast with black throat,
face, and upper breast

Heavy, black bill

Behavior
The plumage of this brightly colored tropical bird actually blends in remarkably well with surrounding foliage, dappled in sun and shade. Largely nonmigratory, small family groups remain year-round within their territory, and nonbreeding adult helpers aid in raising young. Like other jays, eats almost anything from insects and spiders to eggs and young birds to fruits, berries, and seeds. Calls frequently and gregariously a series of raspy *cheh-cheh-cheh* notes.

Habitat
Forages low to the ground in brushy areas and dense riparian growth. Both parents and sometimes helpers build nest of thorny twigs in deciduous trees or shrubs.

Local Sites
From its northern limit along the lower Rio Grande Valley at sites like Santa Ana National Wildlife Refuge, the Green Jay's range extends south to Peru.

FIELD NOTES The Blue Jay, *Cyanocitta cristata* (inset), the most abundant jay in North America, is found year-round throughout eastern Texas. As loud and conspicuous as the Green Jay, its calls include a piercing *jay jay jay* and a musical *weedle-eedle*. Listen as well for its impressive imitation of the Red-shouldered Hawk, a repeated *kee-ah*.

Year-round | Adult

AMERICAN CROW

Corvus brachyrhynchos L 17½" (45 cm)

FIELD MARKS
Black, iridescent plumage overall

Broad wings and fan-shaped tail

Long, heavy, black bill

Brown eyes

Black legs and feet

Behavior
The omnivorous American Crow often forages, roosts, and travels in flocks. Individuals take turns at sentry duty while others feed on insects, garbage, grain, mice, eggs, and baby birds. Known even to crack open shellfish by dropping them onto rocks from above. Because its bill is ineffective on tough hides, crows wait for another predator—or an automobile—to open a carcass before dining. Studies have shown the crow's ability to count, solve puzzles, and retain information. Readily identified by its familiar call, *caw-caw*.

Habitat
Among the most widely distributed and familiar birds in North America. Lives in a variety of habitats. Nests with twigs and grasses in shrub, tree, or pole.

Local Sites
Abundant in the summer in eastern Texas. Still more arrive in winter, pushing the range even farther west.

FIELD NOTES The American Crow's southern counterpart, the Tamaulipas Crow, *Corvus imparatus*, can be found within the U.S. only in one place, Brownsville, Texas. Though an irregular visitor there, look for it in summer in the vicinity of the airport. It is smaller and glossier than the American Crow, with a purplish sheen to its upperparts. Call is a low, froglike croak.

Year-round | Adult

CHIHUAHUAN RAVEN

Corvus cryptoleucus L 19½" (50 cm)

FIELD MARKS
Black overall with puplish gloss

Short, heavy, black bill

Short, wedge-shaped tail

Nasal bristles extend far out on bill; shaggy throat

Concealed white neck feathers

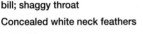

Behavior
An aggressive forager and scavenger, feeds on any number of live prey as well as grains, nuts, fruit, and trash. Uses utility poles scattered throughout desert habitat as way stations for perching, roosting, and nesting. Forms large flocks after breeding that have become huge by winter. In courtship, male puffs out neck feathers and performs aerial maneuvers, then sits next to female to rub bills. Call is a harsh, drawn-out croak, higher pitched than the Common Raven's.

Habitat
Inhabits desert areas and scrubby semiarid grasslands. Nests in tree, shrub, or pole, using sticks, bark, grass, sometimes even barbed wire.

Local Sites
A year-round resident of much of arid West Texas, the Chihuahuan Raven is particularly common in winter in the lower Rio Grande Valley.

FIELD NOTES Though far more widespread to the north, the Common Raven, *Corvus corax* (inset), is found in the same semiarid habitat on the Edwards Plateau and west of the Pecos River as the Chihuahuan. Larger with a longer bill and tail, the Common Raven's deep croak is more likely heard in the mountains than in the mesquite.

Year-round | Adult male

HORNED LARK

Eremophila alpestris L 6¾-7¾" (17-20 cm

FIELD MARKS
White or yellowish forehead bordered by black band, which ends in hornlike tufts on adult males

Black cheek stripes, bill, and bib

Pale yellow to white throat and underparts; brown upperparts

Behavior
The only lark native to North America, forages on the ground, favoring open agricultural fields with sparse vegetation. Feeds mainly on seeds, grain, and some insects. On the ground, the Horned Lark walks or runs, rather than hops, and it seldom alights on trees or bushes. Outside breeding season, these birds organize into flocks, sometimes with longspurs. Song is a weak twittering; calls include a high *tsee-ee* or *tsee-titi.*

Habitat
Prefers open grasslands, dirt fields, sod farms, airports, gravel ridges, and shores. Uses its bill and feet with long hind claws to create shallow depressions for nesting.

Local Sites
In winter, larks are at home on the mudflats of Anahuac National Wildlife Refuge as well as on the arid prairies surrounding the Davis Mountains. They are particularly abundant in summer in the Panhandle.

FIELD NOTES The male Horned Lark performs a spectacular flight display, ascending several hundred feet, circling and singing for a bit, then plummeting headfirst toward the ground, flaring his wings open for landing at the last second. With horns upraised, he then struts for the female, having proven his aerial agility.

Year-round | Adult male

PURPLE MARTIN

Progne subis L 8" (20 cm)

FIELD MARKS
Male is dark, glossy purplish blue

Female has bluish gray upperparts; grayish breast and belly

Long, pointed wings; forked tail

Dark eyes, bill, legs, and feet

Juvenile brown above, gray below

Behavior

Forages almost exclusively in flight, darting for wasps,
bees, dragonflies, winged ants, and other large insects.
Long, sharply pointed wings and a substantial tail allow
it graceful maneuverability in the air. Capable of drinking, even bathing, in flight by skimming just over
water's surface and dipping bill, or breast, into water.
Huge post-breeding colonies roost together in late
summer. Song is a series of liquid, gurgling notes.

Habitat

Common in summer in open habitat near water where
it nests almost exclusively in man-made multi-dwelling
martin houses. Winters in South America.

Local Sites

Arriving in Texas around February, martins are common in central and eastern Texas, essentially wherever
they can find suitable nesting houses.

FIELD NOTES Purple Martins are highly dependent on man-made
nesting houses, which can hold many pairs of breeding adults.
The tradition of making martin houses from hollowed gourds orig-
inated with Choctaw and Chickasaw Indians, who found that this
sociable bird helped reduce insects around villages and crops.
The practice was adopted by colonists and continues to this day.
Martins have accordingly prospered for many generations.

Nonbreeding | Adult

TREE SWALLOW

Tachycineta bicolor L 5¾" (15 cm)

FIELD MARKS
Dark, glossy, greenish blue above

White below

Slightly notched tail

Long, pointed, blackish wings

Juvenile gray-brown above with
dusky wash on its breast

Behavior
Often seen in huge flocks, especially during fall migration, or perched in long rows on branches and wires. Darts over fields or water to catch insects in flight, but switches to diet of berries or plant buds during colder months, when insects are less abundant. The Tree Swallow even preens itself on the wing. Song is a rapid, repeated *chi-veet*.

Habitat
Common to wooded habitats near water, or where dead trees provide nest holes in fields, marshes, or towns. Also nests in fence posts, barn eaves, and man-made birdhouses. Winters along the Gulf Coast.

Local Sites
While most of North America knows the Tree Swallow only as a summer visitor, in Texas it can also be found in wooded areas along the coast in winter. Look as well for the brown-and-white juvenile.

FIELD NOTES The Barn Swallow, *Hirundo rustica*, more common and widespread in summer throughout Texas, shares with the Tree Swallow a deep blue back and a penchant for flying insects. It is set apart though by cinnamon-colored underparts, a reddish brown throat, and a deeply forked tail. By October, it has departed the state completely for Central and South America.

Year-round | Adults

CAVE SWALLOW

Petrochelidon fulva L 5½" (14 cm)

FIELD MARKS
Buffy throat extends around nape and contrasts with dark blue cap and chestnut forehead

Blue-black above with whitish streaks on back and buffy rump

Whitish below with buffy wash on breast and sides; squarish tail

Behavior
Builds elaborate bowl-like nest (opposite) using pellets of mud it collects nearby. A communal nester, it is often found in breeding colonies with Cliff and Barn Swallows. Often rebuilds and reuses same nesting site year after year. Forages over fields and ponds almost exclusively for insects. Song is a disjointed mixture of buzzes, warbles, and chatter.

Habitat
Traditionally nests in caves or sinkholes, allowing young only enough sunlight to feed, but has adapted to man-made structures such as sheltered building walls, bridges, culverts, even drainage pipes.

Local Sites
Its range currently expanding, the Cave Swallow can now be found nesting throughout southern Texas, from caves on the Edwards Plateau to boat-houses on the Gulf Coast.

FIELD NOTES A communal nester under bridges and in culverts with the Cave Swallow, the Cliff Swallow, *Petrochelidon pyrrhonota* (inset), is set apart by its blackish throat and its paler forehead. The Cliff Swallow also uses pellets of mud to make its gourd-shaped nest.

Breeding | Adult

VERDIN

Auriparus flaviceps L 4½" (11 cm)

FIELD MARKS
Yellow face and throat

Gray above, grayish white below

Chestnut-red shoulder patches

Short, black bill

Juvenile brownish gray overall

Behavior
Forages for insects, larvae, spiders, berries, and fruit by actively combing branches and foliage, sometimes suspending itself upside-down in chickadee-like fashion. Male builds multiple nests a season, from which female chooses one to use for brooding. Some are reused in successive years and those not utilized for raising young serve as nighttime roosts or daytime shelters from the blistering southwestern sun. Song is a plaintive three-note whistle, the second note higher-pitched. Repeated *chip* call used to keep small family groups together.

Habitat
Found in mesquite and brushy deserts. Nest is a thick spherical construct up to eight inches wide incorporating sometimes thousands of sticks and twigs.

Local Sites
The Verdin frequents a number of sites along the Rio Grande. Look for it in the Chihuahuan Desert of Big Bend National Park.

FIELD NOTES In general the entrance to a Verdin's first nest of the season faces opposite the direction of the wind in order to allow the sun to bake the interior, desirable for incubating eggs. The entrances of later nests face toward the wind in order to allow breezes to cool the interior, a refuge for parents from the intense heat of the southwestern sun.

Year-round | Adults

CACTUS WREN

Campylorhynchus brunneicapillus L 8½" (22 cm)

FIELD MARKS
Whitish underparts spotted with black, forming a cluster on the upper breast

Brown-and-white streaked on back, barred on wings and tail

Broad white eyebrow; dark brown cap; long decurved bill

Behavior
Often seen in pairs or small family groups, foraging for food on the ground or gleaning insects from vegetation. Also feeds on frogs, small lizards, cactus fruit, and nectar. During courtship, a male wren may chase a visiting female as though she were an intruder, but the female's call of *chur* announces that she is interested in him. The male may then hop stiffly around her and fly to or sing around one of his nest sites, inviting her to inspect it. Its song, heard year-round, is a harsh, low-pitched, and rapid *cha-cha-cha-cha-cha*.

Habitat
Common in cactus country and arid hillsides and valleys with open ground. Large oval nests are woven into spines of cholla cactus or thorny bushes.

Local Sites
The Cactus Wren's unmusical, guttural morning song serves as a wake-up call throughout the desert southwest, especially to campers at Big Bend National Park.

FIELD NOTES North America's largest wren is liable to build its large, easily recognizable nest at any time of the year. Even after young birds have fledged, the nests are still maintained and utilized by the birds as roosting sites.

Year-round | Adult

ROCK WREN

Salpinctes obsoletus L 6" (15 cm)

FIELD MARKS
Gray-brown above, flecked with
white; cinnamon rump

Finely streaked breast on whitish
underparts

Broad, blackish tail band; buffy
tail tips; white undertail coverts
barred with black

Behavior
Small, stocky build allows this wren to move about
readily in closed-in, shrubby, rocky habitats. In
addition, its skull shows a degree of lateral flattening,
allowing it to reach more deeply into crevices than
other species with which it competes for food. Sings
from an exposed perch a variable mix of buzzes and
trills; call is a buzzy *pseee*, audible from some distance.

Habitat
Found in arid and semiarid regions, favoring sunny
scrublands, rocky slopes, and dry washes. Builds nest in
crevice of pile of rocks, sometimes on buildings, always
with trail of tiny rocks leading to entrance.

Local Sites
The Rock Wren is common on the talus slopes in the
foothills of the Rocky Mountains in west Texas.

FIELD NOTES Inhabiting generally wetter
areas than the Rock Wren, the Canyon
Wren, *Catherpes mexicanus* (inset), also
scours rock piles for spiders and insects,
its longer bill compensating for its broader
skull. It is reddish brown overall with a
bright white throat and upper breast.

Year-round | Adult

BEWICK'S WREN

Thryomanes bewickii L 5¼" (13 cm)

FIELD MARKS
Reddish brown or gray upperparts

Whitish underparts

Long, white eyebrow; long decurved bill

Long rounded tail barred lightly in black, edged in white

Behavior
The Bewick's Wren is often seen in pairs. Feeds primarily on ground but also gleans insects and spiders from vegetation. Holds tail high over back, flicking it often from side to side. Male partially builds multiple "dummy" nests, among which female chooses one to complete. Throws head back to belt out its song, a variable, high, thin, rising buzz, followed by a slow trill. Calls include a flat, buzzy *jip*.

Habitat
Prefers brushland and open woods. Inquisitive and tame, the Bewick's Wren can usually be found around human habitation such as ranches and farms. Nests in a variety of cavities from hollow logs to mailboxes.

Local Sites
The reddish-backed subspecies of Bewick's is in serious decline in eastern Texas, but the gray-backed subspecies can still be commonly found farther west at sites like Palo Duro Canyon State Park.

FIELD NOTES Though hard to spot flitting through dense underbrush, the Bewick's eastern counterpart, the Carolina Wren, *Thryothorus ludovicianus* (inset), emits a huge song for such a tiny bird. It is a loud, clear, vivacious *teakettle tea-kettle teakettle*, heard year-round across central and eastern Texas.

Year-round | Adult male

RUBY-CROWNED KINGLET

Regulus calendula L 4¼" (11 cm)

FIELD MARKS
Olive green above; dusky below

Yellow-edged plumage on wings

Two white wing bars

Short black bill; white eye ring

Male's red crown patch seldom
visible except when agitated

Behavior
Often seen foraging in mixed-species flocks, the Ruby-crowned Kinglet flicks its wings frequently as it searches for insects and their eggs or larvae on tree trunks, branches, and foliage. May also give chase to flying insects or drink sap from tree wells drilled by sapsuckers. Calls include a scolding *ji-dit;* song consists of several high, thin *tsee* notes, followed by descending *tew* notes, ending with a trilled three-note phrase.

Habitat
Common in coniferous and mixed woodlands, brushy thickets, and backyard gardens. Highly migratory.

Local Sites
The Ruby-crowned arrives in mid-September and is one of Texas' most common winter birds. Look for it in wooded areas throughout the state.

FIELD NOTES Often in the company of the Ruby-crowned, the Golden-crowned Kinglet, *Regulus satrapa* (inset), can be found in winter as it forages high up in trees. It is set apart by its yellow crown patch and its white eyebrow stripe. The male (inset, bottom) shows a brilliant orange tuft within his yellow crown patch.

Breeding | Adult male

BLUE-GRAY GNATCATCHER

Polioptila caerulea L 4¼" (11 cm)

FIELD MARKS
Male is blue-gray above, female grayer; both are white below

Long, black tail with white outer feathers

Black forehead and eyebrow on male in breeding plumage

Behavior
Often seen near branch tips, the gnatcatcher scours deciduous tree limbs and leaves for small insects, spiders, eggs, and larvae. Sometimes captures prey in flight and may hover briefly. Distinguished by its high-pitched buzz while feeding or breeding. Also emits a querulous *pwee,* intoned like a question. Known to imitate other birds' songs, a surprise to birders expecting this only from mockingbirds and thrashers.

Habitat
Favors moist woodlands and thickets. Male and female together make cup-like nest of plant fibers, spider webs, moss, and lichen on a branch or fork of a tree.

Local Sites
Breeding pairs of Blue-gray Gnatcatchers can be found from eastern pine woods to the Guadalupe Mountains; be careful not to disturb a nest site, as that can cause a couple to abandon it.

FIELD NOTES The gnatcatcher with a brownish back found along most of the Rio Grande is most likely not a Blue-gray, but a female Black-tailed Gnatcatcher, *Polioptila melanura.* The breeding male (inset) is more easily recognized because of his glossy black cap. The species earns its name by the black underside of its tail, edged in white.

Year-round | Adult male

EASTERN BLUEBIRD

Sialia sialis L 7" (18 cm)

FIELD MARKS
Male is bright blue above

Chestnut throat, breast, flanks,
and sides of neck

Female is a grayer blue above,
duller below

White belly and undertail coverts

Behavior

Hunts from elevated perch, dropping to ground to seize
crickets, grasshoppers, and spiders. Has been observed
pouncing on prey spotted from as many as 130 feet
away. In winter, may form small flocks and roost communally, packed into tree cavities or nest boxes. During
courtship, male shows vivid coloring on sides in wing-
waving display beside nesting site. Call is a musical, rising *chur-lee,* extended in song to *chur chur-lee chur-lee.*

Habitat

Found in open woodlands, meadows, and farmlands.
Nests in woodpecker holes, hollow trees, and nest
boxes, competing for spots with introduced species
such as the European Starling and the House Sparrow.

Local Sites

The Eastern Bluebird is most common in the
open woodlands of East Texas and along
the Canadian River in the Panhandle.

FIELD NOTES The Western Bluebird, *Sialia
mexicana* (inset: male, left; female, right), can
be found year-round in the open woodlands of
Guadalupe and Davis Mountains. Like the Eastern, the female is considerably drabber. Unlike
the Eastern, its blue upperparts extend onto its neck and breast.

Year-round | Adult female

AMERICAN ROBIN

Turdus migratorius L 10" (25 cm)

FIELD MARKS
Brick red underparts, paler in
female, spotted in juvenile

Brownish gray above with darker
head and tail

White throat and lower belly

Broken white eye ring; yellow bill

Behavior
Best known and largest of the thrushes, often seen on
suburban lawns, hopping about and cocking its head in
search of earthworms. The American Robin gleans
butterflies, damselflies, and other flying insects from
foliage and sometimes takes prey in flight. Robins also
eat fruit, especially in fall and winter. This broad plant
and animal diet makes them one of the most successful
and wide-ranging thrushes. Calls include a rapid *tut-
tut-tut;* song is a variable *cheerily cheer-up cheerio.*

Habitat
Common and widespread, the American Robin forages
on lawns and nests in shrubs, trees, and even on
sheltered windowsills. Winters in moist woodlands,
suburbs, and parks.

Local Sites
Look for robins in winter almost anywhere in the state,
including suburban backyards. In summer, they are
most common in urban areas to the north and east.

FIELD NOTES The juvenile robin, which can be seen every year
between May and September, has a paler breast, like the female
of the species, but its underparts are heavily spotted with brown.
Look as well for the buff fringes on its back and wing feathers
and short, pale buff eyebrows.

Year-round | Adult

NORTHERN MOCKINGBIRD

Mimus polyglottos L 10" (25 cm)

FIELD MARKS

Gray overall; darker above

White wing patches and outer tail feathers, which flash conspicuously in flight

Long, blackish wings and tail

Short, black bill

Behavior

The pugnacious Northern Mockingbird will protect its territory against other birds as well as dogs, cats, and humans. Has a varied diet that includes berries, grass-hoppers, spiders, snails, and earthworms. An expert mimic, the mockingbird is known for variety of song, learning and imitating calls of many other species and animals. Typically repeats a song's phrases three times before beginning a new one. Call is a loud, sharp *check*.

Habitat

Resides in a variety of habitats, including cities, towns and suburbs. Feeds and nests close to the ground, in thickets, trees, or shrubby vegetation.

Local Sites

The state bird, it is also one of the most widespread and common species throughout Texas.

FIELD NOTES Perhaps the only mimic to truly rival the mockingbird in breadth and variety of imitations is the Gray Catbird, *Dumetella carolinensis* (inset). In addition to its catlike *mew*, the catbird can reproduce calls of other birds, of amphib-ians, even of machinery, and incorporate them into its song. It is a common migrant in central and east Texas.

Year-round | Adult

CURVE-BILLED THRASHER

Toxostoma curvirostre L 11" (28 cm)

FIELD MARKS
Gray-brown above, paler below
with faint spots on breast

Long, dark, strongly curved bill

Long, dark tail has white tips

Orange to yellow-orange eyes

Juvenile bill straighter, eyes paler

Behavior
The most common of Texas' desert thrashers, forages
on the ground by digging small hole into dirt or sand
to expose insects, spiders, or small reptiles. Also eats
cactus fruit, seeds, berries, and snails. Not always able
to extract necessary moisture from arid desert sur-
roundings, the Curve-billed is known to frequent birdbaths, dripping outdoor faucets, or any other available
source of water. Claims territory with a distinctive,
sharp *whit-wheet-whit.* Song varies, but includes low
trills and warbles, often repeated two or three times.

Habitat
Found in semiarid desert brushlands with nearby open
patches. Nests close to ground in shrub or cactus.

Local Sites
The Curve-billed is common along the Rio Grande.
Look for them especially near larger water sources such
as Falcon and Amistad Reservoirs.

FIELD NOTES A common migrant
through the eastern half of Texas, the
Brown Thrasher, *Toxostoma rufum*
(inset), forages like the Curve-billed
by tossing aside leaf litter and digging with
its bill to expose insects and other invertebrates. It is reddish
brown above and heavily streaked below.

Nonbreeding | Adult

EUROPEAN STARLING

Sturnus vulgaris L 8½" (22 cm)

FIELD MARKS
Iridescent black in spring, summer

Buffy tips on back, tail feathers

Fresh fall feathers tipped in white, giving speckled appearance

Yellow bill; in summer its base is pale blue on male, pink on female

Behavior

A social and aggressive bird, the European Starling feeds on a tremendous variety of food, ranging from invertebrates—such as snails, worms, and spiders—to fruits, berries, grains, seeds, and garbage. It probes ground for food, opening its bill to create small holes and expose prey. Usually seen in flocks, except during nesting season. Imitates calls of other species, especially grackles, and emits high-pitched notes, including squeaks, hisses, chirps, and twittering.

Habitat

The adaptable starling thrives in a variety of habitats near humans, from urban centers to agricultural regions. Nests in cavities, ranging from crevices in urban settings to woodpecker holes and nest boxes.

Local Sites

Widespread year-round throughout Texas, the starling is likely to be found in most local parks.

FIELD NOTES A Eurasian species introduced into New York's Central Park in 1890, the European Starling has since spread throughout the U.S. and Canada. Abundant, bold, and aggressive, starlings often compete for and take over nest sites of other birds, including bluebirds, Wood Ducks, a variety of woodpeckers, Tree Swallows, and Purple Martins.

Year-round | Adult

CEDAR WAXWING

Bombycilla cedrorum L 7¼" (18 cm)

FIELD MARKS
Distinctive sleek crest

Black mask bordered in white

Brownish head, back, breast, and
sides; pale yellow belly; gray rump

Yellow terminal tail band

May have red, waxy tips on wings

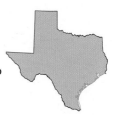

Behavior
Eats the most fruit of any bird in North America. Up to
84 percent of its diet includes cedar, peppertree, and
hawthorn berries and crabapple fruit. Also consumes
sap, flower petals, and insects. Cedar Waxwings are
gregarious in nature and band together for foraging
and protection. Flocks containing several to a few
hundred birds may feed side by side in winter, then
rapidly disperse, startling potential predators. Call is a
thin, high-pitched *zeee*.

Habitat
Found in open habitats wherever berries are available.
The abundance and location of berries influence the
Cedar Waxwing's migration patterns: It moves long
distances only when its food sources run out.

Local Sites
Abundant and gregarious in winter, waxwings arrive
mid-October and sometimes linger until mid-May.

FIELD NOTES One of the more courteous diners in the bird world,
Cedar Waxwings have been known to perch side by side and pass
a piece of food down the row, one bird to the next, until one of them
decides to eat it. If the bird at the end of the line receives the morsel
and is disinclined as well, it is passed right back up the line.

Year-round | Adult

COLIMA WARBLER

Vermivora crissalis L 5¾" (15 cm)

FIELD MARKS

Orange-yellow rump, uppertail coverts, and undertail coverts

Gray-brown above and on flanks

Pale gray hood is topped by rufous crown patch

Distinct white eye ring; gray belly

Behavior

By itself or in a pair, gleans insects and larvae from the branches and vegetation of pine, oak, and juniper trees. Sometimes chases flying insects in direct flight on rapidly beating wings. Male sings frequently by day a high-pitched, upslurred, staccato trill, sometimes ending in clear *tew* note. Call is a loud, sharp *plist*.

Habitat

In Texas, the Colima's habitat is relegated to the pine, oak, and juniper woodlands of the Chisos Mountains. Both sexes build nest on the ground, sheltered by rock overhangs or stream banks, using leaves, grasses, bark, moss, and fur.

Local Sites

This primarily Mexican species nests in the United States only in the higher elevations of the Chisos Mountains in Big Bend National Park. From Laguna Meadow, take the Colima Trail to Boot Canyon and return down the Pinnacles Trail. It's a strenuous hike, but there is great birding to be had along the way.

FIELD NOTES The Colima is rather tame and allows a fairly close approach. If one is heard nearby, but is not visible, try making a *pish* sound with your mouth, a common tool of the birder. The Colima, as well as a number of other small songbirds, is known to respond to such vocalizations.

Year-round | Adult male

NORTHERN PARULA

Parula americana L 4½" (11 cm)

FIELD MARKS
Throat and breast bright yellow
with red patches; white belly

Gray-blue above with yellowish
green upper back

Two white wing bars

Broken white eye ring

Behavior
One of Texas' smallest warblers and a very active
forager that can be observed rightside up or upside
down on branches seeking out larvae; hovering in
search of caterpillars or spiders; or in aerial pursuit of
flying insects. Will fly as far as a mile away to secure a
single piece of Spanish moss for use in its nest. Song
can be heard from treetops during nesting or migration; consists of a rising, buzz-like trill, ending in an
abrupt *zip*.

Habitat
Common in mature coniferous or mixed woods,
especially near water. Prefers to nest in trees covered
with Spanish moss.

Local Sites
Arrives as early as late February. Sabine or Angelina
National Forests are good spots to find the Northern
Parula during breeding season.

FIELD NOTES The Northern Parula's closely
related cousin, the Tropical Parula, *Parula
pitiayumi* (inset: female, top; male, bottom),
occurs in the United States only on Texas's southern-
most coast, south of Matagorda Bay, and in the lower
Rio Grande Valley. It lacks a white eye ring, has a small
black mask, and a diffuse orange breast band on the male.

Immature | "Myrtle"

YELLOW-RUMPED WARBLER

Dendroica coronata L 5½" (14 cm)

FIELD MARKS
Bright yellow rump; yellow patch on sides of breast; pale eyebrow; white throat and sides of neck

Winter birds grayish brown above, white below with brown streaking

Breeding birds have yellow patch on crown, grayish blue upperparts

Behavior
One of the most abundant winter warblers in Texas, darts about branches from tree to tree or in bushes, foraging for myrtle berries and seeds. Often seen in winter in small foraging flocks. Will switch to primarily insect diet before spring migration. Western "Audubon's" race sings soft, repeated *seedle*, fading at end. Songs of eastern "Myrtle" race are higher-pitched, faster, and less musical, including a slow warble and a musical trill. Call a low *chup*, with rising intonation in "Audubon's."

Habitat
Common in fall and winter in brushy and wooded habitats, especially at field edges and on barrier islands. Seeks out areas rich in bayberry or juniper thickets.

Local Sites
The eastern "Myrtle" Yellow-rumped is an abundant winterer across much of Texas, becoming less common west of Edwards Plateau, where the western "Audubon's" subspecies is locally common.

FIELD NOTES The western race of the Yellow-rumped, known as the "Audubon's Warbler," is for the most part similarly marked as the eastern "Myrtle" (described above) but has a yellow throat rather than a white one, and lacks the white eyebrow of the "Myrtle." It can be found in winter west of the Pecos River and on the Llano Estacado.

Year-round | Adult male

GOLDEN-CHEEKED WARBLER

Dendroica chrysoparia L 5½" (14 cm)

FIELD MARKS

Bright yellow face bordered in black, crossed by black eye line

Male has black crown, upperparts, chin, and bib

Female dark olive-green above

White below with black streaking

Behavior

Forages fairly close to ground, hanging chickadee-like from branches as it gleans almost exclusively insects from bark and vegetation. Male sings territorially from high perch all day long a series of four or five harsh, buzzy notes, while female builds nest. She does this by stripping away pieces of bark of an Ashe Juniper tree, and binding them into a tiny cup using spider silk. She then lines the interior with grass, feathers, and fur.

Habitat

A habitat specialist to the utmost, the Golden-cheeked requires not only Ashe Juniper groves for its nest building, but also a dense canopy supported by a variety of other trees, oak, cedar elm, pecan, and river walnut to name a few, for its foraging.

Local Sites

Protected sites still used for nesting by the Golden-cheeked include Meridian and Pedernales Falls State Parks, and Lost Maples State Natural Area.

FIELD NOTES A true Texan, the Golden-cheeked is the only bird of Texas' extensive list that breeds entirely within the state's borders. A sharp decline in the past thirty years has placed this specialty warbler firmly upon the endangered species list. Urban expansion, increased development, and ensuing habitat fragmentation on the Edwards Plateau are cited as major factors.

Year-round | Adult male

PROTHONOTARY WARBLER

Protonotaria citrea L 5½" (14 cm)

FIELD MARKS

Male's head and underparts golden yellow; female duller

Blue-gray wings

Blue-gray tail has white patches; white undertail coverts

Large dark eyes; long black bill

Behavior

Deliberate in plucking insects, larvae, spiders, and seeds from crevices in ground, logs, and trees. Also picks snails and crustaceans right out of water. After arriving on breeding grounds and building several partial nests, male sings incessantly until female arrives and chooses a nest to complete. Song is a series of loud, ringing *zweet* notes; call is a dry *chip*.

Habitat

Common in moist lowland forests, woodlands prone to flooding, and stream banks, but wanders far during migration. Unlike most warblers, nests in tree cavities, nest boxes, or similar crannies, always near water.

Local Sites

Locally common in summer in wooded wetlands of eastern Texas. Brazos Bend State Park has the specific habitat niche the Prothonotary requires to nest. While scanning for birds, watch as well for the park's most conspicuous inhabitant, the American Alligator.

FIELD NOTES The term "prothonotary" originates not with any aspect of the natural world, but with clerks in the Roman Catholic Church, the College of Prothonotaries Apostolic, who wore bright yellow robes for ceremonial purposes.

Year-round | Adult male

SUMMER TANAGER

Piranga rubra L 7¾" (20 cm)

FIELD MARKS

Adult male is rosy red overall

Most females have olive green upperparts, yellow underparts

Some females have overall reddish wash

Large yellowish bill; slight crest

Behavior

With the largest range of the North American tanagers, the Summer Tanager nests in much of Texas. Snags bees and wasps in midair, sometimes even raiding their hives. After catching one, brings the prey back to its perch, then beats it against a branch and wipes the body along bark to remove the stinger before eating. Also feeds on insects, caterpillars, and fruit it deliberately and methodically picks from leaves. Melodic, warbling song is robin-like. Call is a staccato *ki-ti-tuk*.

Habitat

Stays high up in trees of deciduous and mixed forests, especially ones rich in pines and oaks. Female builds nest far up and out on limbs of trees.

Local Sites

The Summer Tanager breeds across most of the central portions of Texas, from the piney hardwoods of Sam Houston National Forest to the cotton-wood thickets of Big Bend National Park.

FIELD NOTES One of the most vividly colored birds to migrate along the Texas Coast in spring, the male Scarlet Tanager, *Piranga olivacea* (inset), like the male Summer Tanager, has a bright red body, but is set apart by his black wings and tail. The female Scarlet Tanager is olive above and yellow below with blackish wings and tail.

Year-round | Adult

OLIVE SPARROW

Arremonops rufivirgatus L 6¼" (16 cm)

FIELD MARKS
Grayish overall with drab olive
wings and tail

Broad, dull brown stripe on either
side of crown

Thin, dull brown stripe through
each eye; white eye ring

Behavior
Usually remains hidden in dense thickets and grassy
undergrowth, foraging low on trees, shrubs, and
ground for seeds and insects. Either gleans food from
foliage or scratches leaf litter with its feet in order to
expose insects. Male sings from well hidden, low perch
a rising series of sharp, repetitive *chip* notes. Calls
include a single *chip* and a high-pitched, buzzy *speee*
given in flight.

Habitat
This Mexican species prefers dense undergrowth and
brushy areas in open woods. Nests near ground in bush
or cactus, using grass, sticks, leaves, bark, and hair.

Local Sites
The Olive Sparrow can be hard to spot year-round in
the dense foliage of sites along the lower Rio Grande,
such as Santa Ana National Widlife Refuge or Bentsen-
Rio Grande Valley State Park.

FIELD NOTES The Canyon Towhee, *Pipilo fuscus*
(inset), largely replaces the Olive Sparrow along the
upper Rio Grande Valley north from Amistad
Resevior. It is gray above, paler on the underparts,
and has a reddish crown sometimes raised into a
crest. A dark central breast spot and fine streaks on the
throat also characterize this inhabitant of semiarid desert canyons.

Breeding | Adult

CHIPPING SPARROW

Spizella passerina L 5½" (14 cm)

FIELD MARKS
Breeding adult shows bright
chestnut crown, white eyebrow,
gray cheek and nape

Winter adult has streaked brown
crown and a brown face

Streaked brown wings and back,
unstreaked gray breast and belly

Behavior
Forages on the ground for insects, caterpillars, spiders,
and seeds. May be found foraging in small family flocks
in fall or in mixed-species groups in winter. Sings from
high perch a one-pitched, rapid-fire trill of dry *chip*
notes. Call in flight or when foraging is a high, hard
seep or *tsik*.

Habitat
The Chipping Sparrow can be found in suburban
lawns and gardens, woodland edges, and pine and oak
forests. Tends to more open areas in winter. Nests close
to the ground in branches or vine tangles.

Local Sites
Widespread throughout the state in winter, the Chipping Sparrow's handsome breeding plumage can also
be found in summer on the Edwards Plateau or in the
Guadalupe and Davis Mountains.

FIELD NOTES Populating many of the same
open woodlands and fields as the Chipping
Sparrow, the Field Sparrow, *Spizella pusilla*
(inset), is widespread during the winter in much of
Texas. Its gray face, light brown crown, and buffy
breast and flanks distinguish it from the Chipping, as well as its
pink bill and distinct white eye ring.

Year-round | Adults

LARK SPARROW

Chondestes grammacus L 6½" (17 cm)

FIELD MARKS
Bold head pattern of chestnut, white, and black

Whitish underparts with dark central breast spot and buffy flanks

Back streaked brown-and-black

White corners on rounded tail

Behavior
Forages in flocks for seeds, insects, and caterpillars, either on ground or in low branches. During courtship, male swaggers on ground and spreads his tail to show off white feathers, then presents female with a twig or stem. A frequent singer, the Lark Sparrow vocalizes on ground, from perch, while flying, and even at night. Song begins with two loud, clear notes, followed by a series of rich, melodious notes and trills, then unmusical buzzes. Call is a metallic *tsip*, mostly heard in flight.

Habitat
For breeding prefers grasslands, roadsides, farms, grassy woodlands, and orchards. Nests on grass, or low in bush or tree. During winter often assembles in flocks in agricultural areas, semiarid grasslands, and larger lowland parks and fields.

Local Sites
A common summer resident throughout most of Texas, the Lark Sparrow can be more difficult to spot in the winter when it retreats farther south.

FIELD NOTES One way to find a Lark Sparrow is to walk softly and slowly through an open field while making a *pish* sound. Once the bird flushes, look for its distinctive chestnut, white, and black head pattern and its white-cornered tail to identify this particular species.

Year-round | Adult

BLACK-THROATED SPARROW

Amphispiza bilineata L 5½" (14 cm)

FIELD MARKS
Black lores, chin, throat, and
upper breast contrast with white
eyebrows and malar stripes

Grayish crown and cheeks,
brownish gray upperparts

Rounded black tail has white
corners that show in flight

Behavior
Usually paired or in a small group, forages for seeds,
spiders, insects, and plant shoots on ground or low in
vegetation. Often walks or runs with tail cocked.
Nesting times vary from year to year, dependent upon
amount of rainfall, hence availability of food. Generally
raises two broods a year. Song begins with two clear
notes, followed by rapid high-pitched trill, heard often
at dawn. Calls are faint, high-pitched, tinkling notes.

Habitat
Inhabits arid and semiarid desert scrublands and rocky
talus slopes. Female builds nest in thorny bush or
cactus with grasses, plant fibers, and hair.

Local Sites
The Black-throated Sparrow is abundant in the Hill
Country and in the Chihuahuan Desert of West Texas
at sites like Big Bend National Park. It is even known to
occur irregularly farther north at Palo Duro Canyon
State Park.

FIELD NOTES Formerly called the desert sparrow, this bird is most
at home under the blazing sun of the southwestern deserts.
Except in summer, it is able to go long stretches of time without
drinking water, as it can usually gain the moisture it needs strictly
from its diet of insects, caterpillars, and plant shoots.

Year-round | Adult

SAVANNAH SPARROW

Passerculus sandwichensis L 5½" (14 cm)

FIELD MARKS

Yellow or whitish eyebrow

Pale median crown stripe on streaked crown

Dark-brown streaked upperparts

White below with brown streaking on chin, breast, and flanks

Behavior

Seen regularly in small, loose flocks, foraging on the ground for seeds and berries in the fall and winter, sometimes scratching like a towhee. Roosts on the ground, packed into a small, tight group. Gathers into large flocks during migration. When alarmed, often runs through grasses on the ground instead of flying. Song begins with two or three *chip* notes, then two buzzy trills. Flight call is a thin *seep*.

Habitat

Common in a variety of open habitats: prairies, marshes, farm fields, grasslands, and even golf courses. In general, breeds farther to the north.

Local Sites

The Savannah Sparrow arrives in Texas in mid-September and sticks around in open areas throughout the state until early April.

FIELD NOTES Because the Savannah Sparrow has few markings that distinctively set it off from similar species, a combination of plumage, habitat, and behavior must be considered to make a definite identification. Staying primarily on the ground in fields or roadsides, the Savannah is one of the most abundant winter sparrows in Texas and is much less secretive than many other similarly streaked sparrows. Its notched tail and its broad whitish eyebrow, usually yellowish in front of the eyes, are also good field marks.

Year-round | Adult

SONG SPARROW

Melospiza melodia L 5¾" (16 cm)

FIELD MARKS
Underparts whitish, with streaks on sides and breast that converge into a dark breast spot

Streaked brown and gray above; broad, grayish eyebrow; broad, dark malar stripe

Long, rounded tail

Behavior
Forages in trees and bushes and on the ground for larvae, fruits, and berries, sometimes scratching ground to unearth grain or insects. One of the most frequent hosts to cowbird parasitism, has learned to drive the menace away from nesting areas. Though for the most part not heard in Texas, melodious song consists of three to four short, clear notes followed by a buzzy *tow-wee* and a trill. Distinctive call is a nasal, hollow *chimp*.

Habitat
Common in winter in suburban and rural gardens, weedy fields, dense streamside thickets, and forest edges. Breeds north and west of Texas.

Local Sites
Song Sparrows arrive in Texas for the winter around mid-November and remain throughout northern parts of the state usually until April.

FIELD NOTES Spreading across most of North America, from the Aleutian Islands of Alaska to the borders of Mexico and eastward along the Atlantic Coast, there are over 30 recognized sub-species of Song Sparrow, all of which have adapted to various specific environments. Pale races, such as *M.m. saltonis,* inhabit arid regions in the Southwest; darker races, such as the eastern *melodia,* inhabit more humid regions; and larger races, such as the Alaskan *maxima,* inhabit oceanic islands.

Year-round | Adult

WHITE-THROATED SPARROW

Zonotrichia albicollis L 6¾" (17 cm)

FIELD MARKS

Broad eyebrow is yellow in front of eye, white or tan behind

Black crown stripes and eye lines

White throat bordered by gray

Streaked rusty brown above, grayish below

Behavior

Almost always seen in a flock in winter, employs the double-scratch foraging method of towhees; that is, it rakes leaf litter with a backward kick of both feet, keeping its head held low and its tail pointed up. Also forages in bushes and trees for seeds, fruit, tree buds, and insects. Often heard before seen, its calls include a sharp *pink* and a drawn out, lisping *tseep*. Its song, sung year-round, is a slow, thin whistle consisting of two single notes then three triple notes: *pure-sweet-Canada-Canada-Canada.*

Habitat

Common in woodland undergrowth, brush, forest edges, and gardens; frequently seen at platform feeders.

Local Sites

Look for the White-throated Sparrow, perhaps even in the company of the White-crowned, at Hagerman National Wildlife Refuge between October and April.

FIELD NOTES Another migrant and winter visitor to Texas is the White-crowned Sparrow, *Zonotrichia leucophrys* (inset). With similar habitat and behavioral characteristics as the White-throated, the White-crowned is distinguished by its lack of yellow in front of the eye and its grayish throat, not as clearly marked off from the breast.

Year-round | Adult male "Slate-colored"

DARK-EYED JUNCO

Junco hyemalis L 6¼" (16 cm)

FIELD MARKS
Variable dark upperparts

White belly and undertail coverts

Gray or brown head and breast, sharply set off in most races

White outer tail feathers in flight

Juveniles of all races are streaked

Behavior
Scratches on ground and forages by gleaning seeds, grain, berries, insects, caterpillars, and fruit from plants. Occasionally gives chase to a flying insect. Forms flocks in winter, when males may remain farther north or at greater elevations than juveniles and females. Song is a short, musical trill that varies in pitch and tempo. Calls include a sharp *dit,* and a rapid twittering in flight.

Habitat
Winters in a variety of habitats, often in patchy wooded areas. "Red-backed" subspecies breeds in mixed woods at higher elevations of Guadalupe Mountains.

Local Sites
A number of Dark-eyed Junco subspecies are scattered in winter throughout the northern portions of Texas: "Slate-colored" (opposite) to the east; "Oregon" (below) to the west; and "Gray-headed" in the Panhandle and around the Pecos River.

FIELD NOTES The "Oregon Junco" is the race most likely encountered in winter in west Texas. The male (inset, bottom) has a black hood and gray rump; the female (inset, top) has a dark brown hood and dark rump. Both are characterized by buffy brown back and flanks, and white outer tail feathers.

Nonbreeding | Adult male

MCCOWN'S LONGSPUR

Calcarius mccownii L 6" (15 cm)

FIELD MARKS

Buff-edged back feathers

Whitish below; pied upper breast on male, buffy on female

Pinkish bill with dark tip

White tail marked by inverted, dark T-shape, visible in flight

Behavior

Forms large flocks in winter, often in company of Horned Larks. Forages on ground for seeds, insects, and caterpillars, and makes daily visits to watering holes such as irrigation canals. Undulating flight alternates between rapid wing beats and brief glides. Calls include a short, dry rattle and a *poik*, given either by itself or doubled.

Habitat

In winter, found in plowed fields, dry lake beds, and dirt fields. Breeds in dry shortgrass prairies of northern Great Plains. Though population is now stable, range has shrunk considerably since the 19th century.

Local Sites

McCown's Longspurs arrive on the High Plains in late October, where they remain until mid-March. Their movement to plains and prairies farther south is irregular and sporadic, but they can usually be found on the Llano Estacado all the way to the northwestern part of the Edwards Plateau.

FIELD NOTES Often found in barren fields with little vegetation amid of large flock of Horned Larks, look for the McCown's chunkier body, its shorter, mostly white tail, its slightly darker plumage, and its thicker bill.

Year-round | Adult male

NORTHERN CARDINAL

Cardinalis cardinalis L 8¾" (22 cm)

FIELD MARKS
Male is red overall, black face

Female is buffy gray-brown tinged
with red on wings, crest, and tail

Large, conspicuous crest

Cone-shaped, reddish bill;
blackish on juvenile

Behavior
Forages on ground or low in shrubs mainly for seeds,
leaf buds, berries, and fruit. Nonmigratory and aggressive in defending its territory, a cardinal will attack not
only other birds, but also itself, reflected in windows,
rear-view mirrors, chrome surfaces, and hubcaps. Sings
a variety of melodious songs year-round, including a
cue cue-cue, a *cheer-cheer-cheer*, and a *purty-purty-
purty*. Listen for courtship duets in spring and summer.

Habitat
Year-round resident in gardens and parks, woodland
edges, streamside thickets, and practically any environ-
ment that provides thick, brushy cover. Nests in forks
of trees and bushes, or in tangles of twigs and vines.

Local Sites
The cardinal is abundant and conspicuous
throughout most of Texas, except west of
the Pecos River, where it is less common.

FIELD NOTES The Pyrrhuloxia, *Cardinalis
sinuatus* (inset: female, top; male, bottom),
found in thorny brush and mesquite thickets
of arid southwest Texas, resembles a female
cardinal in its conspicuous crest and reddish
tinges on a gray body, but its bill is yellow and
sharply curved like that of a parrot.

Year-round | Adult male

PAINTED BUNTING

Passerina ciris L 5½" (14 cm)

FIELD MARKS
Adult male has purplish blue
head; red eye ring, breast, and
rump; bright green back

Female is bright green above,
paler yellow-green below

Juvenile resembles female, but
duller overall

Behavior
Forages alone or in a pair, hopping on ground or low in
trees and shrubs for insects, caterpillars, and seeds.
Males are feisty and may draw blood—or even fight to
the death—to defend territory. Courtship display consists of male spreading wings and tail, puffing up body
feathers, and performing before female in a herky-jerky
motion. Female carries out work of building nest and
incubation. Male sings from exposed perch a high-
pitched, musical warble; call is a loud, rich *chip*.

Habitat
Locally common in streamside thickets and moist,
brushy lowlands. Nests close to ground in dense foliage
of bush, tree, or vine tangle. Declining primarily due to
illegal trapping and trading in Mexico.

Local Sites
Arriving in April, Painted Buntings nest throughout
much of Texas. Pedernales Falls State Park is a good
spot to listen for the male's song.

FIELD NOTES Almost as striking as the male Painted
Bunting is the male Indigo Bunting, *Passerina cyanea*
(inset), a bright blue overall, slightly darker on the
head. The female is brown, with dusky streaks on
her flanks, and can resemble a sparrow. They are
abundant in summer in east Texas away from the coast.

Year-round | Adult male

RED-WINGED BLACKBIRD

Agelaius phoeniceus L 8¾" (22 cm)

FIELD MARKS

Male is glossy black with bright red shoulder patches broadly edged in buffy yellow

Females densely streaked overall

Pointed black bill

Wings slightly rounded at tips

Behavior

Runs and hops while foraging for insects, seeds, and grains in pastures and open fields. The male's bright red shoulder patches are usually visible when it sings from a perch, often atop a cattail or tall weed stalk, defending its territory. At other times only the yellow border may be visible. Territorially aggressive, a male's social status is dependent on the amount of red he displays on his shoulders. Song is a liquid, gurgling *konk-la-reee,* ending in a trill. Call is a low *chack* note.

Habitat

Breeds in colonies, mainly in freshwater marshes and wet fields with thick vegetation. Nests in cattails, bushes, or dense grass near water. During winter, flocks forage in wooded swamps and farm fields.

Local Sites

The Red-winged is common to abundant year-round in wetlands throughout Texas. Numbers increase in winter when migrants join the resident population.

FIELD NOTES Usually less visible within large flocks of singing males, the female Red-winged (inset) is streaked dark brown above and has dusky white underparts heavily streaked with dark brown. In winter you may find a whole flock of just females.

Breeding | Adult

EASTERN MEADOWLARK

Sturnella magna L 9½" (24 cm)

FIELD MARKS
Yellow below, with black V-shaped
breast band, paler in winter

Black-and-white striped crown
with yellow supraloral area

Brown above streaked with black

White outer tail feathers in flight

Behavior
Flicks its tail open and shut while foraging on the
ground, feeding mainly on insects during spring and
summer, seeds and agricultural grain in late fall and
winter. Generally solitary in summer, the meadowlark
forms small flocks in fall and winter. Male known to
brood while female starts second nest. Often perches
on fence posts or telephone poles to sing a clear,
whistled *see-you see-yeeer.* Flight call is a buzzy *drzzt.*

Habitat
Prefers open space offered by grasslands, pastures,
meadows, and farm fields. Female constructs a domed
nest on ground, woven into the surrounding grasses.

Local Sites
Listen for the rich, musical song of the Eastern
Meadowlark in the coastal prairies at sites like Anahuac
or Brazoria National Wildlife Refuges, or further inland
at Caddo National Grassland.

FIELD NOTES The Eastern Meadowlark's counterpart,
the Western Meadowlark, *Sturnella neglecta*
(inset), is nearly identically plumaged, but with a
lighter brown back and yellow on its throat
extending farther onto the malar area. Its
territorial song, a rich, bubbling, repeated *shee-o-e-lee,*
can be heard at nesting grounds in the Panhandle.

Year-round | Adult

COMMON GRACKLE

Quiscalus quiscula L 12½" (32 cm)

FIELD MARKS
Plumage appears all black; in good light, shows glossy blue hood, bronze body, purple tail

Long, wedge-shaped tail

Pale yellow eyes

Female plumage not as iridescent

Behavior
Rarely seen outside of a flock, this grackle moves to large, noisy, communal roosts in the evening. During the day, mainly seen on the ground in a group, feeding on insects, spiders, grubs, and earthworms. Also wades into shallow water to forage for minnows and crayfish. Known to feast on eggs and baby birds. Courtship display consists of male puffing out shoulder feathers to make a collar, drooping his wings, and singing. These birds produce sounds like ripping cloth or cracking twigs. Call note is a loud *chuck*.

Habitat
Prefers open spaces provided by farm fields, pastures, marshes, and suburban yards. Requires wooded areas, especially conifers, for nesting and roosting.

Local Sites
Abundant throughout eastern portions of Texas, the Common Grackle has increasingly expanded westward into urban areas since the 1950s.

FIELD NOTES The shorter-tailed Brewer's Blackbird, *Euphagus cyanocephalus* (inset: male, left; female, right), is a winter visitor throughout Texas, more so to the west. The male has a greenish blue gloss; the female is a dark gray-brown overall.

Year-round | Adult male

GREAT-TAILED GRACKLE

Quiscalus mexicanus L 18" (46 cm) Female L 15" (38 cm)

FIELD MARKS

Large with very long tail

Male iridescent black overall with purple sheen on head and back

Female dark brown overall, paler on throat and breast

Yellow eyes, duller on female

Behavior

In winter, may join large groups numbering in the thousands. Not a territorial bird, flocks forage together, locating rich food sources and sharing their finds. Individuals spend less time on alert for predators, since all glance around for danger. Male's courtship pose consists of wings drooped, tail spread, and bill pointed skyward. Dominant males gather a harem of females, with whom they mate and whom they defend against advances by other males. Voices are harsh, with varied calls, including clear whistles and loud *clack* notes. Courtship wing shaking produces strange rattling.

Habitat

Common and increasing in open flatlands with scattered groves of trees, and in marshes and wetlands.

Local Sites

Abundant in urban areas across Texas, Great-taileds in the north are less common outside of cities. Look for nesting colonies in river valleys throughout the southern brush country and the coastal prairies.

FIELD NOTES In the marshes of Texas' upper Gulf Coast at sites like Anahuac National Wildlife Refuge, resides a similarly plumaged bird with just as long a tail, but slightly smaller and with brown eyes. This is the Boat-tailed Grackle, *Quiscalus major*, best identified by its song, a harsh, repeated *jeeb*.

Year-round | Adult male

BRONZED COWBIRD

Molothrus aeneus L 8¾" (22 cm)

FIELD MARKS
Male has greenish bronze gloss on head and body, bluish sheen on wings and tail

Female dull blackish overall

Distinct red eyes

Heavy black bill

Behavior
Finds insects by flipping over rocks with bill. Also follows cattle to feed on flushed prey. Mostly seen in pairs during breeding season; in winter, forms large flocks and roosts communally in trees by night. Male sings from exposed perch a quiet, guttural gurgling to attract females. Both genders fluff out neck ruffs during breeding season, producing hunchbacked appearance. Like other cowbirds, deposits eggs in active nests of other species, leaving responsibility of brooding to host and often destroying host eggs in the process.

Habitat
Often found close to the activities of man, such as agricultural areas and ranchlands. Breeds in open woodlands and brushy scrublands.

Local Sites
The Bronzed Cowbird is a common breeder in Texas along the length of the Rio Grande and is currently expanding its range as far north as Lubbock.

FIELD NOTES The Brown-headed Cowbird, *Molothrus ater* (inset), flourishes throughout Texas, adapting to newly cleared lands and exposing new songbirds to its parasitic nesting strategy. The female lays up to 40 eggs a season in nests of host birds, often destroying the eggs of endangered species such as the Black-capped Vireo.

Year-round | Adult male

BULLOCK'S ORIOLE

Icterus bullockii L 8¼" (22 cm)

FIELD MARKS
Male has bold orange face and
underparts; black crown, back,
tail, throat patch, and eye line

Female has yellow face, throat,
and breast; drab olive wings,
back, and tail; grayish belly

Large white wing patches

Behavior
Forages in trees and bushes for insects, berries, and
fruit. Inserts long, sharply pointed bill into crevices to
probe for ants, mayflies, and spiders. In breeding
season, male chases female with such actions as wing-
drooping and repeated bowing, all while displaying
brilliant orange plumage. Pairs are noisy and conspicuous, and spend much time together, but mate for
only one season. Song is variable, but always composed
of whistles and harsher notes; call is a clear, harsh *cheh*,
sometimes given in a series.

Habitat
Breeds in open wooded areas, especially those rife with
deciduous trees. Female weaves grasses into intricate
hanging baskets or pouches for nests.

Local Sites
Look for this striking bird by itself or in a small family
group in summer at Buffalo Lake National Wildlife
Refuge or surrounding areas of west Texas.

FIELD NOTES The Bullock's Oriole was once considered the same
species as the Baltimore Oriole, *Icterus galbula*, which passes
through most of east Texas in migration. The two hybridize
where their ranges overlap in the Great Plains, though the male
Baltimore has a full black hood and much less white in his wings
than the male Bullock's. The female Baltimore shows considerably more orange overall than the female Bullock's.

Year-round | Adult male

HOUSE FINCH

Carpodacus mexicanus L 6" (15 cm)

FIELD MARKS
Male's forehead, bib, and rump typically red, but can be orange or, occasionally, yellow

Brown streaked back, white belly, streaked flanks

Female streaked dusky brown on entire body

Behavior
A seed eater, the House Finch forages on the ground, in fields and in suburban yards. Often visits backyard feeders. Seen in large flocks during winter. Flies in undulating pattern, during which squared-off tail is evident. Male sings a conspicuously lively, high-pitched song consisting of varied three-note phrases, usually ending in a nasal *wheer*. Calls include a whistled *wheat*.

Habitat
Adaptable to varied habitats, this abundant bird prefers open areas, including suburban parks and areas where it can build its cup-like nest on buildings. Also nests in shrubs, trees, cacti, or on the ground.

Local Sites
The House Finch is fairly common year-round in east and west Texas. Not until the 1990s did the ranges of the native western population and the introduced eastern population meet in central Texas, though both are still rare there.

FIELD NOTES The female House Finch (inset) is grayish brown overall and heavily streaked on her entire body. Pairs can often be found during breeding season, and small family groups after nesting, but this gregarious bird forms large foraging flocks for the winter, sometimes with other species.

Year-round | Adult male "Black-backed"

LESSER GOLDFINCH

Carduelis psaltria L 4½" (11 cm)

FIELD MARKS
Male black on hood, back, and
tail; bright yellow below

Female greenish olive above, dull
yellow below

White wing bars and edges to
tertial and primary flight feathers

Behavior
Pairs or small flocks forage for seeds and insects in
bushes, shrubs, and weedy fields. Commonly visits
birdbaths and outdoor faucets in the semiarid southwest, as diet of primarily seeds does not provide a lot of
moisture. Male feeds female while she is brooding and
pairs may stay together for life. Song, given by male in
flight, is a lively series of warbles and *swee* notes. Call,
given often by small flocks, is a *tee-yee tee-yer*.

Habitat
Found in dry brushlands and open woodlands with
scattered trees. Also tends to areas of human habitation
to take advantage of artificial sources of water. Female
builds nest in bushes or trees, sometimes in tall weeds.

Local Sites
Lesser Goldfinches nest along the length of the Rio
Grande and into the Hill Country at sites like Lost
Maples State Natural Area. Around El Paso, look
for the green-backed form of this bird.

FIELD NOTES The widespread American
Goldfinch, *Carduelis tristis*, is a common winterer throughout Texas. The winter male (inset) is easily distinguished from his smaller cousin by his light
brownish upperparts, black forehead, and white belly.
The female is told apart by her grayish belly, neck, and breast.

Breeding | Adult male

HOUSE SPARROW

Passer domesticus L 6¼" (16 cm)

FIELD MARKS
Breeding male has black bill, bib, and lores; chestnut eye stripes, nape, back, and shoulders

Winter male less distinct

Female has brown back, streaked with black; buffy eyestripe; and unstreaked grayish breast

Behavior
Abundant and gregarious year-round. Hops around, feeding on grain, seeds, and shoots, or seeks out bird feeders for sunflower seeds and millet. In urban areas, begs for food from humans and will clean up any crumbs left behind. In spring and summer, multiple suitors will chase a possible mate in high-speed aerial pursuit. Females choose mate mostly according to song display. Singing males give persistent *cheep*.

Habitat
Found in close proximity to humans. Can be observed in urban and suburban areas and in rural landscapes inhabited by humans and livestock. Nests in any sheltered cavity, often usurping it from another species.

Local Sites
Abundant wherever humans habitate, House Sparrows flock in the most heavily urbanized areas.

FIELD NOTES Also known as the English Sparrow, the House Sparrow was first introduced into North America through New York's Central Park in the 1850s, in an effort to populate the park with all the birds mentioned in Shakespeare's plays. It has since spread across the continent to become one of the most successful bird species in North America, to the detriment of many native species. Ironically, its numbers are declining precipitously in its native England.

Mostly Brown

 Fulvous Whistling-Duck, 15

 Mottled Duck, 25

 Blue-winged Teal, 27

 Ruddy Duck, 35

 Plain Chachalaca, 37

 Pied-billed Grebe, 43

 American Kestrel, 81

 King Rail, 83

 Greater Roadrunner, 127

 Eastern Screech-Owl, red morph, 129

 Great Horned Owl, 131

 Common Pauraque, 135

 Cave Swallow, 179

 Curve-billed Thrasher, 203

 Cedar Waxwing, 207

 House Sparrow, 261

Mostly Brown and White

 Canada Goose, 19

 White-tailed Hawk, 75

 Red-tailed Hawk, 77

 Killdeer, 91

 Willet, 99

 Yellow-billed Cuckoo, 125

 Burrowing Owl, 133

 Northern Flicker, 151

 Horned Lark, 173

 Cactus Wren, 187

 Rock Wren, 189

 Bewick's Wren, 191

 Yellow-rumped Warbler, 213

 Chipping Sparrow, 225

 Lark Sparrow, 227

 Savannah Sparrow, 231

 Song Sparrow, 233

 White-throated Sparrow, 235

 McCown's Longspur, 239

The main entry for each species is listed in **boldface** type and refers to the text page opposite the illustration.

A check-off box is provided next to each common-name entry so that you can use this index as a checklist of the species you have identified.

ACKNOWLEDGMENTS

The Book Division would like to thank the following people for their guidance and contribution in creating the *National Geographic Field Guide to Birds: Texas*

Tom Vezo:
Tom Vezo is an award-winning wildlife photographer who is widely published throughout the U.S. and Europe. Located out of Green Valley, Arizona, he specializes in bird photography but photographs other wildlife and nature subjects as well. He is also a contributor to the *National Geographic Reference Atlas to the Birds of North America*. For a look at more of his images, find his gallery at tomvezo.com.

Brian E. Small:
Brian E. Small has been a full-time professional wildlife photographer specializing in birds for more than 15 years. In addition, he has been a regular columnist and Advisory Board member for *WildBird* magazine for the past 10 years. An avid naturalist and enthusiastic birder, Brian is currently the Photo Editor for the American Birding Association's *Birding* magazine. You can find more of his images at www.briansmallphoto.com.

Cortez C. Austin, Jr.:
Cortez Austin is a wildlife photographer who specializes in North American and tropical birds. He has a degree in zoology and has done graduate work in conservation, ecology, and microbiology. An ardent conservationist, he has donated images, given lectures, and written book reviews for conservation organizations. In addition he has published numerous articles and photographs in birding magazines in the United States. His photographs have also appeared in field guides, books, and brochures on wildlife.

Bates Littlehales:
National Geographic photographer for more than 30 years covering myriad subjects around the globe, Bates Littlehales continues to specialize in photographing birds and is an expert in capturing their beauty and ephemeral nature. Bates is co-author of the *National Geographic Photographic Field Guide: Birds,* and a contributor to the *National Geographic Reference Atlas to the Birds of North America*.

Larry Sansone:
An active birder since 1960, Larry Sansone began photographing wildlife in the early 1970s. His pictures are published in field guides and magazines in the U.S. and Europe. He was a technical advisor to the first edition of the *National Geographic Field Guide to the Birds of North America*, and he is photo editor of *Rare Birds of California* by the California Bird Records Committee.